SAN JUAN ISLAND'S

GREY TOP INN

SOUPS AND STEWS COOKBOOK

TABLE OF CONTENTS

ACKNOWLEDGMENTS

The editors of this cookbook wish to thank all of those who have contributed their time and talents to the completion of the book as you who use it see it in its final form. Many have given many hours of work and put much of their personal talent into its completion.

Our thanks to those cooks who have helped us with some of their own recipes. First, our thanks to professional chef Greg Atkinson, a former San Juan Island resident, and to a favorite chef and owner of the Duck Soup Inn here on San Juan Island, Gretchen Allison. Others who have given us recipes used in the book are Carolyn Blakeway, Jane Buck, Nancy Jo Cavenagh, Barbara Fagan, Mary Guard, Ina and Jane Mullis, Bill Paterson, Laurie Paull, Mary Jane Pitt, Lainey Volk, Kathryn Ward, Irene Warner, Nadine Wells, Ann Wiese and Peg Wilson. Your three editors have, of course, added to the wealth with recipes of their own.

We are so very pleased to have had help, through their artistry and experience, with the cover of the book from our own Sam Connery, a well known artist who lives here on the island, and Bryn Barnard, who is responsible for the printing which appears thereon. We thank the Publisher and Editors of the <u>At Home Magazine</u> for the use of their excellent map of the San Juan Islands which is on our back cover. And we want to thank Louise Dustrude for her work in proofreading all the materials and her son Tim Dustrude, of Dustrude Design, for his work in preparation of the book for printing, and, my very great personal thanks to Curt Widdoes, for his computer expertise in getting this book completed.

And for myself, as Chairman of the Editorial Committee, my thanks for all their help to Winifred Fairfax and Nancy Lindenberg, my co-editors.

Marcella Widdoes, Editorial Chairman

INTRODUCTION

This book is happily dedicated to San Juan Island's old Grey Top Inn, and the memories of many islanders here of the meals served at the "Grey Top" before there were many really good places on the island for groups to gather for social or other activities. It became a place where the community could provide meals as well as other social services for the disabled and older members of the community, for whom many of the chores of everyday living, like preparing meals, had become too difficult. The "Grey Top Inn", as it became known, is located at the County Fairgrounds, which is on the edge of downtown Friday Harbor, the small commercial center of the island, where the ferry docks and the private sailboats and power boats sit at rest in the picturesque marina. Throughout those early years of growth on the island, the little Grey Top became the focal point for all sorts of gatherings, and a place where older residents could get a good, hot meal, and transportation to and from home. It was a place to meet, make friends, get together with friends, and enjoy the day. Many friendships grew out of the gatherings at the old Grey Top.

Although the old Grey Top Inn has been replaced by the new Mullis Community Senior Center, it still sits in its place as before at the Fairgrounds, and it will always be a part of this island's history. May the spirit of those times continue to be the spirit of all these San Juan Islands, warm and helpful to those around us, as we hope the pages of this cook book will bring warmth and pleasure to the kitchens and dining rooms of those who use it.

Bon appetit from the Editorial Staff and all those who contributed their time and effort to this production.

CHILLED SOUPS

AFTER DINNER LEMON SOUP

A beautiful soup to serve at the end of a big, celebrative dinner, this is a palate satis-
fier, as well as delicious. Scandinavians serve it at the end of a meal for dessert
with thin almond cookies.

3 tbsps. butter
3 tbsps. flour
1 or 2 small lemons (grate the peel and set aside,
  then squeeze the juice and set aside)
3 egg yolks, well beaten
3 tbsps. sugar

Meringue
2 egg whites
2 tbsps. sugar
cinnamon

Melt the butter and blend in the flour. Cook together for a few minutes, then add 1
quart of water a little at a time, stirring until smooth and thickened. Add the grated
lemon peel and boil for about 10 minutes. Remove from stove. Add the lemon
juice to the soup, then add a ladle of the soup to the well beaten egg yolks and
sugar. Return to the mixture, which is still off the stove. Stir until smooth and
pour into soup bowls. Beat the egg whites stiffly, adding the sugar gradually. Put a
spoonful in each soup bowl, sprinkled with the powdered cinnamon. This soup can
be served either hot or well chilled.

Serves 4 or 5

CHILLED CELERY SOUP

1 medium leek (white and pale green parts only) chopped
  (about 1/2 cup)
6 cups chopped celery (about 12 ribs)
1 medium onion, chopped
1 tbsp. olive oil
1 small boiling potato, unpeeled and finely chopped
2 cups water
1 medium clove garlic put through garlic press
salt and freshly ground pepper to taste
1 tsp. paprika

Wash and dry leek in cold water. Cook celery, onion, leek and garlic in oil in heavy
pot over moderate heat, stirring frequently, until ingredients are softened, about 10
minutes. Add remaining ingredients except paprika and simmer, covered, until celery and potatoes are tender, about 10 minutes. Sprinkle in paprika and stir to blend.
Puree in batches in a blender until smooth taking care with hot mixture, then force
through a fine mesh sieve into a bowl, pressing hard on solids, then discarding
them. Place bowl in refrigerator to cool, stirring occasionally. Serve chilled or at
room temperature, sprinkling a touch of paprika on top of each bowl.

Serves 4

BLENDER CUCUMBER SOUP

2 medium cucumbers, peeled and sliced
  (save 4 thin slices for garnish)
1 cup buttermilk
1/2 cup light cream
1 small green onion, cut up using some of the green
fresh parsley
1/4 tsp. garlic salt
salt and pepper to taste
1/2 tsp. white wine tarragon vinegar
1/2 cup sour cream

Put all ingredients into the blender except the sour cream and parsley. Blend. Add sour cream and gently fold into the mixture. Chill. Garnish each bowl with a reserved slice of cucumber and a sprig of parsley.

Serves 4

COLD APPLE SOUP

What a delicious summer treat this beautiful soup is! Serve for dessert or just for fun!

8 apples
2 cups apple juice
2 lemons, juice only
1 tbsp. sugar or to taste
1 cinnamon stick

2 cups orange juice
2 cups whipping cream
3 tbsps. Cointreau or
Triple Sec
1/2 tsp. vanilla

Peel, core and quarter 6 apples. Combine with apple juice, lemon juice, sugar, cinnamon stick and vanilla in large saucepan. Cover and cook over medium heat until apples are very soft, about 20 minutes. Let cool, then cover and refrigerate 24 hours. Remove cinnamon stick. Add orange juice and whipping cream to apples and puree in batches in blender until smooth. Pour into chilled tureen. Shred remaining 2 apples (unpeeled) and stir into soup along with liqueur. Serve immediately.

Serves 8

COLD AVOCADO SOUP

A deliciously quiet soup with a colorful and very tasteful red caviar topping.

1 large or 2 medium ripe avocados
1 cup chicken broth, canned or homemade
1 cup heavy cream
2 tsps. lemon juice
salt and white pepper to taste
red caviar or other, or chopped fresh dill atop a sprinkle of paprika

Peel the avocado and put into a blender or through a food mill. Heat the pureed avocados with the chicken broth, stirring until smooth and blended. Add the cream, lemon juice, salt and pepper. Stir gently but thoroughly. Chill well and serve sprinkled lavishly with the red or other caviar or use the suggested small bit of chopped fresh dill over a tiny sprinkle of the paprika.

Serves 4

COLD BEET SOUP

This is a strictly American version of cold beet soup, popularly known as Borscht where it is found, because this one is made with several ingredients strange to Borscht, especially the garnish at the top of each bowl.

7 small beets, washed
2 cups chicken broth or stock
1 large Idaho potato, peeled and
quartered

Salt
1 tbsp. wine vinegar
1 tsp. chopped fresh tarragon
1 cup sour cream

Leave the roots and an inch of the tops on 6 of the beets. Boil the beets in salted water until tender. Peel, slice, and put in a pan with the chicken stock. Cook the potato very slowly in salted water until very soft. Drain, add to the beets and bring to a boil. Puree the broth, beets and potato in a food mill, blender or food processor, small batches at a time. Reheat the soup with salt to taste, wine vinegar and chopped tarragon. Cool a little and mix in the sour cream. Chill thoroughly. Before serving, peel and grate the remaining beet. Serve the soup in cups with a dollop of sour cream on top and a sprinkle of the fresh, grated beet on top of that.

Serves 4

JEWISH FRUIT SOUP

1/2 cup finely diced oranges
1/2 cup finely diced pineapple
1/2 cup finely diced peaches
1/2 cup finely diced strawberries
1/2 cup finely diced rhubarb
1 cup sugar
salt to taste
1 qt. water
1/2 cup sour cream

Simmer the fruits, sugar and salt with the water for 10 minutes. Chill the resulting fruit mixture. Just before serving add the sour cream and blend thoroughly. If desired garnish with a fresh strawberry, or a sprig of fresh parsley.

STRAWBERRY SOUP

This soup is also a dessert type soup, but in the hot weather it makes a lovely change from tea and pastries at an afternoon tea with crisp, thin lemon or almond cookies to accompany.

2 (10 oz.) pkgs. frozen strawberry
    halves, partially thawed
1/4 cup sugar
2 1/2 tbsps. quick cooking tapioca

Dash of salt
1 tbsp. fresh lemon juice
1/2 cup very small pieces
fresh grapefruit and orange

Press strawberries through a sieve or ricer or blend until smooth in a blender. Place the pureed fruit into an enamel or stainless steel saucepan. Add 2 cups water and the sugar, tapioca and salt. Let stand for 5 minutes, then cook and stir over medium heat until mixture comes to a full boil. Remove from heat immediately and add lemon juice.
Cool, stirring mixture after 15 minutes' rest. Chill. Add grapefruit and orange pieces just before serving.

Serves 4

TOMATO AND DILL BISQUE

2 medium onions, chopped
1 clove garlic, sliced
2 tbsps. butter
4 large tomatoes (2 lbs.) peeled and cubed
1/2 cup water
1 chicken flavored bouillon cube
2 1/4 tsps. fresh or 3/4 tsp. dried dill weed
salt and white pepper to taste
1/2 cup mayonnaise

In a 2 qt. saucepan over medium heat cook onions and garlic in butter 3 minutes. Add remaining ingredients, except mayonnaise, cover and simmer 10 minutes. Remove from heat and cool. Place half at a time in blender and cover. Blend until uniform. Pour into a large bowl. Stir in the mayonnaise carefully until fully blended. Cover and chill overnight in the refrigerator.

Serves 4-5

BLENDER GASPACHO

1 spine of celery (with leaves) cut in pieces
1 carrot cut in pieces
1 medium onion, cut in pieces
1/2 green pepper cut in pieces (other raw vegetables may be substituted or added as
    desired — lettuce, zucchini cucumber seeded and peeled, etc.)
1 large clove garlic, pressed (or more if desired)
1 tbsp. Worcestershire Sauce (Lea & Perrins recommended)
1 tbsp. olive oil (optional)
1/2 tsp. basil or 1 tbsp. if using fresh
4 or 5 cups tomato juice
salt and freshly ground pepper to taste

Put all ingredients together in blender (if tomato juice will not all fit, add remainder in a larger vessel after blending), and blend at medium speed only until vegetables are coarsely ground, not pureed. Chill for at least one hour before serving. Serve with garlic croutons if desired (although this is not the Hispanic way).

Serves 6

HISPANIC STYLE BLENDER TOMATO SOUP

This soup is not Gaspacho, but it is a tasty, tomato flavored sister.   Great on a hot summer day.

2 lbs. fresh tomatoes, blanched, peeled, seeded and chopped, or
   1 (15 oz.) can tomato soup plus half a can of water
1 cup peeled cucumber, chopped
3 tbsps. strong flavored onion, finely chopped
1 1/2 tbsps. red wine vinegar
1 1/2 tbsps. olive oil (optional)
2 cloves garlic, pressed
salt to taste
1/4 tsp. cayenne pepper (or to taste)
1/2 cup sour cream (plus more for garnish)

Blend all ingredients, adding sour cream last. Chill for at least one hour. Garnish with a very thin 2 or 3 slices of cucumber, skin intact, with a dollop of sour cream on top.

Serves 6 to 8

COLD CHERRY SOUP

This is a lovely soup to serve on a very hot day as an ice cold starter for a meal in the German manner, or as a liquid dessert in the Scandinavian way.

1 1/2 pounds pitted sweet or sour cherries
1 cup red wine
3 cups water
1/4 to 1/2 cup sugar or more, according to cherries and taste
1/2 tsp. grated orange peel
1 1/2 tsps. arrowroot
whipped cream or tiny macaroons

Put the cherries, red wine, 3 cups of water, sugar and orange peel in an enameled pan. Cook over medium heat until cherries are soft, about 10 minutes. Puree in a blender or put through a sieve. Thicken the soup with arrowroot mixed with a little of the cooled juice. Add more sugar if necessary. Cook for a minute or two until thickened and clear. Chill. Serve with a dollop of whipped cream on each bowl or a macaroon or two in the bottom.

Serves 6

COLD MELON SOUP

1/2 large cantaloupe or Persian melon, cut in cubes
1/2 large honeydew or honey ball, cut in one inch balls
1 1/2 cups orange juice
1/4 tsp. ground cinnamon
3 tbsps. fresh lime juice
fresh mint sprigs for garnish.

Place cantaloupe cubes, ground cinnamon, and 1/2 cup orange juice in a blender and puree. Combine remaining 2 cups orange juice and lime juice. Stir into puree. Add honeydew balls. Pour mixture into a bowl and cover. Refrigerate at least one hour before serving. Serve soup garnished with sprigs of fresh mint.

Serves 6

SWEDISH FRUIT SOUP

Try serving this in place of fruit for a special breakfast (maybe with a glass of champagne!)

2 tbsps. quick cooking tapioca
2 cups unsweetened pineapple juice
1 tbsp. sugar
1/2 tsp. lemon peel

1 (10 oz.) package frozen
  red raspberries, thawed
1/2 cup diced orange sections

Combine the tapioca and one cup of the pineapple juice in a saucepan. Let stand for 5 minutes. Cook and stir over medium heat until the mixture comes to a full boil. Remove from heat. Add the sugar, remaining pineapple juice and lemon peel; stir to blend. Cool; then cover and chill. Before serving, fold in the raspberries and orange sections.

Serves 4

CLEAR SOUPS

CONSOMME MADRILENE

3 cups homemade beef stock,* or 2 cans beef consomme
2 small tomatoes (blanched in hot water, skins removed and reserved)
2 sprigs finely chopped parsley
4 sprigs finely chopped chives
1 tbsp. Port wine, either tawny or red

Heat the beef stock or consomme. Cut peeled tomatoes in half, squeeze juice and seeds together with the reserved skins into the consomme. Remove skins, dice tomatoes and set aside for garnish. Simmer consomme for about 10 minutes. Strain off the solids, then add reserved chopped tomatoes, chives, parsley and Port to the liquid and heat, but not to boiling.

This soup may be served either hot or cold.

Serves 4

*See recipe for Beef Stock in section on Stocks.

JAPANESE CLEAR SHRIMP SOUP

5 fresh shrimp
1 small onion, sliced paper-thin
sliced carrot with serrated edges
1 stalk celery
salt to taste
pinch of sugar

dash of soy sauce
1 egg, beaten
thin pieces of lemon peel
juice of 1/2 lemon
4 sprigs parsley

Simmer the shrimp, onion, carrot, celery, salt, sugar and soy sauce in 4 C. or more of water. Simmer until vegetables are barely tender. Remove the celery, add a spoonful of broth to the well- beaten egg, mix and add to the soup. When serving, put a few pieces of lemon peel with a dash of lemon juice and a sprig of parsley in each cup. This should be served in small thin Oriental bowls.

Serves 4.

An elegant, simple and distinguished Japanese soup. It seems incredible that a soup with so few and such simple ingredients should have flavor, but it does indeed.

CLAM AND TOMATO BROTH
WITH CURRIED CLAM CUSTARD

1 pint clam juice
1 pint tomato juice
1/2 bay leaf
1/2 tsp. grated lemon peel

Heat clam and tomato juices with the bay leaf and grated lemon peel. Check the seasonings – commercial tomato juices vary greatly in flavor and seasonings – and add more if necessary. Remove the bay leaf and serve with tiny pieces of curried clam custard.

CURRIED CLAM CUSTARD

1 egg
2 egg yolks
3/4 tsp. salt
1 1/2 tsp. curry powder

1 can minced clams (drain and
 save juice)
1 tbsp. sherry

Beat the eggs thoroughly. Add 1/2 C. of the clam juice. Add the salt, curry powder, clams and sherry. Beat well and pour into a greased shallow pan, about 1/2-inch deep. Set in a larger pan of hot water, cover and steam over low heat for 25 minutes, or until a knife inserted into the custard comes out clean. This can be made ahead of time and chilled. To serve, cut into small diamonds or other shape with vegetable cutters. Serve 3 or 4 pieces in each soup bowl.

Serves 4 or 6.

A celestial, unstereotyped, delicate and spicy beginning for a meal. Fancy vegetable cutters can be used to cut the custard into shapes, or cut into 1/2 inch diamonds or squares with a knife.

JAPANESE EGG DROP SOUP

1 large onion, sliced
3 tbsps. butter
2 cans beef bouillon, diluted, or
    2 cups homemade bouillon.
1/4 cup soy sauce
salt and pepper to taste
4 eggs

Sauté the onion in butter in a deep skillet, until glazed. Add the bouillon diluted with water, or homemade bouillon, with the soy sauce. Adjust seasonings. Simmer for about 5 minutes. Lower the heat more, so there is only the barest movement of the broth. Add the raw eggs to the broth, cover and poach for 3 to 5 minutes. Serve, allowing 1 egg to each serving.

Serves 4.

An authentic recipe. Friends back from three years in Japan will have no other. It is a soothing and restorative soup, a panacea. May be served with bread.

OLD SOUTH ALMOND SOUP

This soup is a very old and very unusual Southern soup. If you can't find orange flower water, try the substitutes listed here.

3/4 cup almonds, blanched and finely ground
1 cup celery, finely chopped
2 tbsps. cornstarch
1 qt. orange juice
1/2 tsp. orange rind, finely grated
2 cups water
1 tsp. orange flower water (or substitute 1/2 tsp. ground nutmeg,
   and 1/4 tsp. almond extract - or to taste)
salt to taste

Cook celery in the water with a little salt and the grated orange rind until celery is tender. Blend cornstarch with a little water and add for thickening. Quickly add the ground almonds and the orange juice. Sprinkle in the nutmeg and add the almond extract if using, or the orange flower water if you were lucky enough to find some.

Serves 4

SWISS BEER SOUP

1 cup cubed French bread, crusts removed
3 tbsps. oil
1 large onion, chopped
1 large garlic clove, minced
12 oz. (1 1/2 cup) beer
3 cups chicken broth*
freshly ground pepper to taste
2 tbsps. minced fresh parsley
1 1/2 to 2 cups grated Gruyere cheese
1 tsp. paprika

Preheat oven to 400° F. Arrange bread cubes on baking sheet and toast until brown, turning to color evenly.

Preheat broiler. Heat oil in large saucepan over medium heat. Add onion and sauté until onion is limp and golden. Stir in bread cubes. Add beer and chicken broth, and bring to boil. Add pepper and parsley and blend well. Ladle soup into individual heatproof bowls. Divide cheese evenly and sprinkle over soup. Sprinkle with paprika. Run under broiler until cheese is golden brown.

Serves 4 to 6

* If using canned chicken broth, add an additional 1/2 cup water to avoid oversalting, or use bouillon cubes. If using packaged croutons, look for unsalted and nongreasy croutons.

TOMATO SOUP ALLA TORINESE

This northern Italian soup is now very popular and known as tomato-basil in the U.S.

1 lb. sun ripened tomatoes, or 1 (16 oz.) can plum tomatoes, chopped
1 large clove garlic, minced or pressed
4 or 5 leaves fresh basil, finely chopped
1 tbsp. fresh lemon juice
1 tbsp. sugar
1 tsp. salt or to taste
1/4 tsp. white pepper
2 tbsps. butter
2 tbsps flour
4 cups chicken broth, or stock, heated

In a saucepan combine tomatoes with juice, garlic, basil, lemon juice, sugar, salt and pepper. Cover and bring to a boil. Lower heat and simmer 30 minutes. Pour into blender and puree. Melt butter in same saucepan. Blend in the flour, then gradually add chicken broth stirring constantly until well blended. Cover and cook over low heat for 10 minutes. Add tomato puree to broth and cook over low heat 10 minutes longer. Serve hot or thoroughly chilled.

Serves 6

CREAM SOUPS

CREAM OF FRESH VEGETABLE SOUP

2 heads of lettuce, any kind, chopped coarsely
1 large handful fresh spinach (or 1/2 pkg. chopped frozen if necessary)
4 medium carrots, unpeeled and scrubbed
1 medium onion, chopped coarsely
1 bunch scallions, sliced
1 medium potato, skin on, chopped coarsely
1/4 small cabbage, chopped coarsely
2 stalks celery with leaves, sliced
5 cups chicken broth plus 2 cups water
1/2 tsp. dried dill (or 1 tbsp. fresh chopped)
1/8 tsp. each basil and tarragon
1 tbsp. fresh parsley chopped finely
salt and freshly ground pepper to taste
juice of 1 lemon

Simmer all ingredients in the broth and water until vegetables are just tender. Strain solids from broth and put through a blender a few cups at a time, returning puree to the pot with the broth. Heat until hot enough to serve, or, if desired, prior to final heating you may add any of the following combinations:

> 2 egg yolks beaten with 1 cup cream, mixed with 1/2 cup burgundy or
> 2 egg yolks beaten with 1 cup cream, mixed with 1 or 2 cloves garlic, mashed
>   and sauteed in a little oil, or
> 2 egg yolks beaten with 1 cup cream, mixed with 1/2 cup medium or dry sherry

Heat until any egg yolk and cream mixtures have had time to cook, then add to final soup the juice of one lemon.

Any combination of mild vegetables may be used in substitution for some of those above, but be sure they are mild in flavor. Otherwise the character of this delicate soup will be all wrong.

Serves 6 - 8

CREAM OF ONION SOUP ENGLISH STYLE

1 large onion, sliced
1/4 cup butter
6 cups chicken stock or broth
1/4 tsp. white pepper
1 1/4 cups heavy cream

Saute' the onion in the butter over medium heat, stirring for 10 minutes or until the onion is golden. Add the stock and pepper and simmer, covered, for 30 minutes. Puree in a blender, then return to the pot. Stir in the cream by adding a small amount of the soup to the cream in another pan until the cream has been thinned out and heated. Then add all to the original pot and heat over very low heat until heated through.

Serve hot, with or without croutons.

Serves 6-8

CREAM OF SPINACH SOUP

1 lb. spinach (or 1 cup frozen)
3 tbsps. butter
1 small onion peeled and grated
1 large clove garlic minced
2 cups milk
2 cups chicken or vegetable stock
3/4 tsp. salt or to taste
1/2 tsp. dried tarragon
1 small grating of a fresh nutmeg

Pick over and wash the fresh spinach and place it (or the frozen if using) in a saucepan and cook about 6 minutes covered. Drain and put through a strainer or a blender. Melt the butter in a saucepan and add the grated onion and the garlic, and saute' 3 minutes. Stir in the flour and cook until blended, then gradually stir in the milk and stock. Season with the tarragon and the nutmeg. Add the spinach and heat the soup well. Serve sprinkled with freshly grated Parmesan cheese or a little grated carrot or sprig of fresh parsley.

Serves 4

CREAM OF TURNIP SOUP

2 cups very small, young, white turnips (not big winter ones), peeled and diced
1 quart beef broth
1 cup heavy cream
salt and freshly ground black pepper to taste
2 egg yolks, beaten
1 Tbsp. butter

Cook the turnips in the beef broth until tender. Drain, reserving the liquid. Rub turnips through a sieve or food mill, or puree in a blender. Return turnips to the reserved liquid and bring the pot to a boil, then remove from the heat, add the cream and season with salt and pepper to taste. Reheat the soup but do not boil. Remove from heat and stir in the egg yolks and butter. Do not return to the boil, but serve hot.

Serves 6

SPINACH AND CLAM SOUP

2 pkgs. chopped frozen spinach
1 cup heavy cream
1 cup light cream
2 cups clam juice
1 1/2 tsp. dried dill weed
juice of 1/2 lemon
ground black pepper to taste
freshly grated nutmeg

Allow spinach to thaw slightly, then add to 1/2 cup boiling water, cover and cook for 3 to 4 minutes. Puree in a blender, return to the pan, add the heavy cream, light cream, dill weed and clam juice. Stir well and heat, then add lemon juice and pepper to taste.

This soup may be served either hot or cold, with a sprinkle of the freshly grated nutmeg on top of each serving.

Serves 4

18

CHEESE VELVET SOUP

This is a lovely, quietly delicious cheese soup, soft on the palate. Consider a light meal to follow.

8 ozs. Brie cheese
2 ribs celery, finely chopped
2 carrots, finely chopped
1/2 onion, finely chopped
8 tbsps. butter
8 tbsps. flour

2 1/2 cups chicken broth
1 bay leaf
1 tsp. thyme
salt and pepper to taste
1/2 cup whipping cream
chopped chives for garnish

Cut away rind on cheese and discard. Cut cheese into cubes and set aside. Saute' vegetables in butter over medium heat. Add flour and blend, making a roux. When butter is absorbed and the mixture thick, heat the broth, add to the mix, and stir until thick again. Add bay leaf and thyme. Slowly add the cheese, stirring until melted. Add cream and heat thoroughly. Garnish each serving with a sprinkle of the chopped chives.

Serves 4 to 6

CHESTNUT SOUP WITH COGNAC CREAM

2 tbsps. (1/4 stick) butter
1 tbsp. olive oil
1 celery stalk, chopped
1 small carrot, chopped
1/2 medium onion, chopped
1 tsp. minced fresh thyme, or 1/4 tsp. dried
4 cups canned, low-salt chicken broth
2 cups boiled chestnuts (see recipe below)
** or 2 cups vacuum-packed chestnuts (about 10 oz.) halved**

1/4 cup whipping cream
2 tsps. Cognac
pinch of salt

Melt butter with oil in heavy, large saucepan over medium heat. Add celery, carrot, onion and thyme. Saute' until vegetables are tender, about 10 minutes. Add broth and chestnuts. Cover partially and simmer until chestnuts are very tender, about 30 minutes. Puree soup in batches in blender. Season to taste with salt and pepper. Cover and chill.
This part of the recipe may be prepared one day ahead.

Whisk cream, Cognac and pinch of salt in medium bowl until thickened but not stiff. Set aside. Bring soup to simmer over low heat. Ladle into bowls. Swirl spoonful of Cognac cream into each bowl and serve.

CHESTNUTS
You may substitute whole, cooked chestnuts for vacuum-packed chestnuts available at specialty food stores, some supermarkets or on line. (Williams-Sonoma)

Cooked chestnuts: One pound fresh chestnuts. Makes about two cups.

Using small, sharp knife, cut an X in each chestnut. Cook chestnuts in large saucepan of boiling water until just tender, about 15 minutes. Working in batches, use slotted spoon to transfer several chestnuts to work surface. Remove hard shell and papery brown skin while chestnuts are still warm.

Serves 4

COLOMBIAN PEANUT SOUP

Try this soup on your family first, (or serve to guests whom you know are willing to submit to an experiment), since it is an unusual dish. Great fun for the adventurous appetite!

2 tbsps. butter
1 medium onion, chopped
1 large bunch of celery, trimmings and very top parts only
6 cups chicken stock
3 scant cups soft, cream style peanut butter
1 cup heavy cream
1 tsp. cinnamon
2 tbsps. tomato puree
1/2 tsp. lemon juice
1/8 tsp. thyme
1/4 cup dry sherry
1/4 to 1/2 tsp. sugar
fresh chopped tarragon or parsley for garnish

Saute' the onion and trimmings of celery in the 2 tbsps. butter unil limp. Add the chicken stock and simmer until vegetables are soft. Puree in a blender with the soft peanut butter.
Return to saucepan and add the cream, cinnamon, tomato puree, lemon juice and thyme.
Simmer over low flame until soup is thick and hot, stirring often. Add the sherry and then the sugar, being careful to taste for sweetness. Serve sprinkled very sparingly with the chopped tarragon or parsley.

Serves 6 to 8

CREAMY CAULIFLOWER SOUP

Be sure you use a very good chicken broth, because it is the foundation of this delicious soup.

1 medium head of cauliflower, cut into tiny flowerets
1/4 cup sweet butter
2/3 cup chopped onion
2 tbsps. flour
2 cups chicken broth
2 cups light cream
1/2 tsp. Worcestershire sauce (Lea & Perrins, please)
3/4 tsp. salt or to taste
1 cup grated sharp Cheddar cheese
fresh chives or parsley, chopped

Cook cauliflower in boiling salted water. Drain, reserving liquid. Melt butter. Add onion and cook until soft. Blend in flour alternately with the broth, stirring until smooth and all broth has been added. Cook, stirring constantly, until mixture comes to a boil. Stir in 1 cup liquid drained from cauliflower, adding water if necessary to make 1 cup. Then add the cream, Worcestershire sauce and salt. Add the cauliflower and heat to boiling. Stir in the cheese. Serve hot, sprinkled with chopped chives or parsley.

Makes about 2 quarts, serving 4 to 6

LIMA BEAN SOUP

This simple soup is wonderful, and one of the 3 editors' favorites:

1 cup dried lima beans
4 slices bacon, diced
1/2 cup onion, chopped
1 stalk celery, chopped
1 cup boiling water
1 carrot, peeled and chopped
salt and pepper to taste
1 can (12ozs.) evaporated milk

Soak the beans overnight, drain and rinse. Put in a casserole with all the ingredients except the canned milk and mix. Bake at 325° F., covered, for two hours. Add the milk at the last just to heat. If you like lima beans you will love this little soup!

Serves 4

22

MONGOL CREAM SOUP

20 ounces frozen peas
1 carrot, chopped
1/2 tsp. salt
1 bay leaf
2 cups tomato juice or V-8 juice
2 stalks celery, chopped

1 large onion, chopped
1 garlic clove, minced
2 tbsps. butter
2 tsps. curry powder
1 can beef consomme' (10 oz)
1 cup light cream

Cook carrot in tomato or V-8 juice. Add peas, salt and bay leaf and cook 3-4 minutes. Saute' onion, garlic and celery in the butter, adding the curry powder. Pour in consomme' and heat. Combine all ingredients except the cream, remove the bay leaf and chill. Add the cream just before serving, mixing well.

Serves 6-8

NORWEGIAN CUCUMBER SOUP

1 tbsp. butter
1/2 medium onion, chopped
1 carrot, sliced
4 cups celery, with leaves, chopped
3 cucumbers, peeled and diced
1/4 tsp. thyme
1/2 tsp. tarragon
6 cups chicken broth

In top of a double boiler, saute' the onion, carrot and celery in the butter until limp. Add the cucumber, thyme, tarragon and chicken broth, and cook, covered, until vegetables are soft. Puree in a blender and return to the double boiler over hot water.

2 eggs
1 cup heavy cream
2 tbsps. dry sherry
1/8 tsp. lemon juice

Beat the eggs with the cream, sherry and lemon juice. Gradually add a cup of the hot soup to the mix, stirring constantly, then slowly add the egg mixture to the soup, stirring until well blended and creamy. Serve hot, sprinkled with a little sweet paprika on top of each serving.

Serves 8

PARSLEY AND POTATO SOUP

4 medium potatoes, peeled and cut into 1/2" cubes
3 or 4 strips of thin sliced bacon
1 medium onion, chopped
2 cups chicken stock
2 cups milk or light cream
2 cups chopped parsley

Cook potatoes until tender. Drain, saving water. Cook bacon pouring out most of the oil.
Saute' onion in the bacon pan. Return the potatoes to the pot with the chicken stock and milk. Heat slowly. Put parsley, onions and half the potatoes in the blender, along with the liquid in which the potatoes were cooked. Blend. Combine the blended potatoes, the remainder of the potatoes together with salt and pepper. Serve with a spot of butter on top. Lovely, light green color gives final product pleasing eye appeal.

Serves 6

PUMPKIN SOUP

This pumpkin soup is delicious, and a little less complicated to make than the curried one also presented in this book.

2 tbsps. butter
1/4 cup chopped green pepper
2 tbsps. chopped onion
1 large sprig parsley
1/8 tsp. thyme
1 bay leaf
1 (8oz.) can tomatoes - 1 cup
1 (1 lb.) can pumpkin
2 cups chicken broth or stock
1 tbsp. flour
1 cup milk
1 tsp. salt or to taste
1/8 tsp. white pepper

Melt butter in large saucepan. Add green pepper, onion, parsley, thyme and bay leaf. Cook 5 minutes. Add tomatoes, pumpkin and chicken broth. Cover and simmer 30 minutes, stirring occasionally. Press mixture through food mill or wire strainer. Blend together flour and milk and stir into soup. Add salt and pepper and cook, stirring frequently, until mixture comes to a boil. Serve immediately.

Serves 6

SWEDISH MUSHROOM SOUP

3 tbsps. butter
1 lb. fresh mushrooms, with stems, thinly sliced
1/2 tsp. salt
1/4 tsp. ground white pepper
1/3 cup flour
2 quarts beef or chicken broth (or bouillon)
1 cup heavy cream
1 tsp. lemon juice
1/4 cup dry white wine
salt and freshly ground white pepper to taste

Melt butter in 3-4 quart heavy saucepan over low heat. Add mushrooms and saute'
over low heat until mushroom juices begin to flow. Pour juices into a 2 cup measure and set aside. Stir the 1/2 tsp. salt, 1/4 tsp. pepper and the flour into drained
mushrooms. Add broth to mushroom juice to make 2 cups. Stir into mushroom
mixture. Stir in 6 cups remaining broth. Over high heat, cook and stir until soup
thickens, almost 5 minutes. Stir in cream and lemon juice. Add salt and white pepper to taste. Stir in white wine. Serve hot.

Serves 8

VICHYSSOISE

4 leeks, white part and 1" of green only, sliced
1 medium onion, sliced
4 tbsps. butter
5 medium potatoes, peeled and sliced thin
1 quart chicken broth, or water
1 tbsp. salt
3 cups milk
2 cups heavy cream
finely chopped green onion or chives for garnish

Brown the leeks and onion in the butter, then add the potatoes, chicken broth (or
water) and salt; boil for 35 or 40 minutes. Puree in blender. Chill well. Add the
milk and heavy cream and blend. Season to taste. Sprinkle with chopped chives or
green onion and serve cold.

Serves 6-8

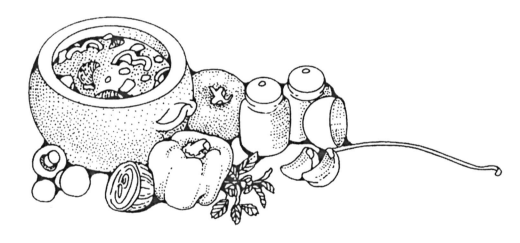

VEGETABLE SOUPS

BLACK BEAN SOUP WITH APPLES
AND GARAM MASALA

1/4 to 1/2 cup butter
2 large onions, peeled and diced
2 tbsps. fresh ginger, chopped
2 carrots, finely diced
3 celery stalks, finely diced
2 apples, such as Fuji, peeled and finely diced
2 to 3 cups hard apple cider, or substitute white wine
3 qts. chicken or beef stock or broth
2 red bell peppers, roasted, peeled and diced
4 cups cooked black beans
1 tbsp. dry currants
1/2 tsp. hot chili flakes (optional)
1/3 cup fresh parsley, chopped
salt and pepper to taste
a good squeeze of lemon or lime juice
1 tsp. garam masala spice mix (or make your own*)
crushed peanuts and cilantro creme* for garnish

In a large stainless steel pot melt butter and saute' onions until brown around the edges. Add ginger and continue to brown until ginger is fragrant. Heat cider to boiling to displace the alcohol, then add carrot, celery and apple along with cider to the pot. Add stock, peppers, black beans, currants, chili flakes (if using), parsley, pepper and salt to taste. Simmer until beans get really soft and begin to thicken the soup. Add more stock or broth if needed. Add lemon or lime juice and the garam masala. (At this point a handful of parsley and cilantro may be added if desired.) Spoon into warm bowls and garnish with crushed peanuts and cilantro creme*.

* See glossary for these recipes
    garam masala
    cilantro creme

Serves 6 to 8

"AVGOLEMONO" GREEK EGG AND LEMON SOUP

8 cups clear chicken broth, canned or homemade
4 eggs
1 cup sliced mushrooms
1 1/2 tbsps. brandy
juice of 2 lemons (or 3 small limes)

Heat broth in large saucepan, but do not boil. Beat eggs until light and foamy. Add lemon juice and beat some more. (Or put eggs and lemon juice in blender and blend one minute.) Add 2 cups of the hot broth to the egg-lemon mixture, gradually, stirring thoroughly. Then add the egg-lemon-broth mixture to the rest of the broth.

Saute' the mushrooms lightly in a little butter (not more than 1 tbsp.) and add to the soup. Serve immediately.

Serves 6-8

BORSCHT

The term Borscht is a Russian dish, basically a kind of stew made with duck, beef and sausages, cut small and cooked in meat stock and blended with 'kwas' or beet juice and sour cream, and garnished with shredded, cooked leeks, beets and celery root. The term may also be applied to a soup, originally of Russia, Poland and Balkan countries, made of beets, water, onions, various meats depending on the region — in Poland spareribs, in Russia beef, and in various of the regions cabbage may also be part of the recipe. It is historically a winter soup, but has become popular cold, served in summer with sour cream as a garnish, with which we in the U. S. are all familiar. We present here a sample of each type:

COLD BORSCHT WITH SOUR CREAM

5 medium beets, peeled and diced, or canned diced beets may be used
juice of one lemon
1 cucumber, peeled, seeded and cubed
2 spring onions, with tops and bottoms, chopped
sour cream

Cook the beets in 1 quart of water with the lemon juice for 30 to 40 minutes, or until beets are tender. If using canned this step may be eliminated. Reserve the liquid from whichever one is used, and serve it in chilled bowls with some of the beets, cucumber, chopped spring onions and a good dollop of sour cream in each bowl. Can be kept in the refrigerator for several days.

Or a simpler version eliminates the other vegetables as follows:

1 1/2 cups sliced beets and juice (15 oz. can)
3/4 cup chicken broth
1 1/2 tbsp. lemon juice
1 tbsp. chopped onion
salt to taste
2 tbsps. sour cream

Blend all ingredients except sour cream. Stir in sour cream and chill. Serve with a dollop of sour cream atop each bowl.

Each of these recipes serves about 4.

UKRAINIAN BORSCHT
For this recipe refer to section of   Meat and Vegetable Soups

BORSCHT WITH BEETS AND CABBAGE

This is a representation of the type of borscht served frequently in kosher restaurants, which are described as "with improvements".

1 quart soup stock made with 2 large
  beef bones with plenty of beef, boiled
1/4 lb. chopped celery
1/4 cup chopped green pepper
1 clove garlic, sliced thin
1 piece bacon rind, well aged
1 (1 lb.) can tomatoes
1/2 tsp. freshly ground black pepper
sour cream

1 tbsp. minced parsley
2 medium potatoes, diced
1/4 medium cabbage,
  sliced thin
1 cup julienne beets (use
  canned and save the juice)
1 cup carrots, scraped and
  cut julienne

Put the soup stock in a pot with 1 quart of water, celery, green pepper, garlic, bacon rind, tomatoes, black pepper and parsley. Bring to a boil, cook for 1/2 hour, add the potatoes, cook another 1/2 hour, add the cabbage and cook for 20 minutes more. Add the beets, juice and carrots and cook for 10 minutes more. This is better the second or third day.
Serve warm topped with a dollop of sour cream.

Serves 8 to 10

BROCCOLI SOUP WITH VEGETABES

3/4 cup chopped onion
3/4 cup chopped celery
2/3 cup chopped carrots
8 ozs. to 1 lb. fresh broccoli chopped
1 1/2 cups chicken broth
1 tbsp. butter
1/2 tsp. rosemary
1/2 tsp. salt (or to taste)
1 cup light cream
1/4 tsp. lemon juice

Saute the onion and celery in the butter. Cook the broccoli and carrots in 1 cup of the chicken broth. Blend the onion, celery, broccoli and carrots with the rosemary and salt, and heat, adding the other 1/2 cup of chicken broth after mixing in the cup of cream. When all the soup is well mixed add the lemon juice. Serve hot, but do not boil.

Serves 4

BROCCOLI AND CARROT SOUP

3/4 cup chopped onion
3/4 cup chopped celery
2/3 cup chopped carrots
8 ozs. to 1 lb. chopped fresh broccoli
1 1/2 cups chicken broth
1 tbsp. butter
1/2 tsp. rosemary
1/2 tsp. salt
1 cup light cream
1/4 tsp. lemon juice

Saute' onion and celery in the butter. Cook broccoli and carrots in 1 cup of the chicken broth. Blend the onion-celery and broccoli-carrots with the rosemary and salt. Heat with added 1/2 cup chicken broth, cream and lemon juice.

Serves 3 to 4

CREAM OF EGGPLANT SOUP

This eggplant soup is easier to make than the one presented in our section Meat and Vegetable Soups, very different from it, and serves a larger number of people.

6 tbsps. (3/4 stick) butter
3 cups diced onion
3 cups diced celery
2 large eggplants, unpeeled and diced
3 cups diced potatoes
1 tsp. curry powder or to taste
1/2 tsp. thyme
1/2 tsp. sweet basil
8 cups chicken stock, or broth
4 cups whipping cream

Melt butter in a 6 qt. pot. Saute' onion, celery, eggplant and potatoes. Add seasonings and cook, uncovered, over medium heat, stirring frequently, until potatoes are tender, about 10 to 15 minutes. Stir in stock and cook, uncovered, over medium heat until mixture begins to thicken, about 45 minutes. Remove from heat, add the cream and serve immediately.

Serves 12 to 16

FRESH TOMATO SOUP

This soup is outlined here with two other variations, and each of the three versions is delicious.

1 small onion, finely chopped
3 tbsps. butter
6 medium, ripe tomatoes, peeled,
   seeds removed, and chopped
salt and freshly ground black
   pepper to taste

1/4 tsp. baking soda
1/4 to 1/3 tsp. dried sage
1 cup heavy cream
sour cream for garnish

Saute' the onion in the butter until soft and limp. Add the tomatoes, salt and pepper to taste, baking soda, and sage. Cook for 10 to 12 minutes, or until thickened and paste like. Remove from the heat and stir in the cream. Taste for seasoning, and reheat. Serve hot, garnished with a spoonful of sour cream sprinkled with chopped parsley. This may also be refrigerated and served cold in the same manner.

For Puree of Tomato Soup:
  Puree the tomato mixture and cream in a blender for a smooth soup.

For Tomato Soup with Orange:
  Omit the sage and add 1/4 tsp. thyme, 1 tsp. grated orange rind, and
  3 tbsps. concentrated orange juice.

Each soup serves 4

GOLDEN SWEET POTATO/CARROT SOUP

1 tbsp. butter
1 tbsp. fresh ginger root, chopped thickly for easy removal
1 large shallot, minced
2 large carrots, sliced
1 large sweet potato, peeled and cut into chunks
1 1/2 to 2 cups chicken broth
1 cup half and half or whole milk
dash of freshly ground nutmeg
1/2 tsp. curry powder

Melt butter in medium saucepan. Add ginger root and shallot and saute' over low heat until ginger is tender, about 5 minutes. Add carrots, sweet potato and 1 cup chicken broth. Increase heat and simmer, covered, until vegetables are very tender, about 30 minutes. Remove pieces of ginger root. Cool slightly. Remove vegetables to food processor or blender with some of the liquid, and puree'. Return mixture to pan. Add half and half, remaining 1/2 cup chicken broth, nutmeg and curry powder. Adjust the spices and amount of liquid. Simmer until heated through.

Serves 2 to 3 heartily
Double the recipe for 8

IRENE'S ZUCCHINI SLICES

If you have ever run out of ideas about how to make a 'different' dish from fresh zucchini when it is in season, try this easy, fast and delicious curry flavored, creamy 'bisque'. And the author says that you can substitute broccoli, carrots, or other favored vegetables in place of the zucchini.

4 cups zucchini slices
chicken broth to cover (about 3 cups)
1 3 oz. package cream cheese, softened
1/2 tsp. curry powder (or to taste)
salt and pepper to taste

Cover zucchini slices with the broth and cook until just tender. Blend with remaining ingredients. Reheat carefully, being careful not to overheat, and serve with perhaps a dollop of sour cream and a sprinkle of dried or fresh dill on top.

Serves 4 to 6

LAINEY'S BAKED GARLIC SOUP

Butter a 3 quart baking dish. Preheat oven to 375 degrees F.

2 cups fresh tomatoes, diced
4-5 summer squash, sliced
1 (15 oz. can) garbanzo beans,
  not drained
2 large onions, sliced
1/2 green pepper, diced
1 1/2 cup dry white wine

4-5 cloves fresh garlic, minced
1 large bay leaf
2 tsps. salt
1 tsp. basil
1 tsp. paprika

1 1/4 cup Monterey Jack cheese, grated
1 cup Romano cheese, grated
1 1/4 cups heavy cream (use canned fat-free half and half for
  healthier version)

Combine first 11 ingredients (tomatoes through paprika) and place in baking dish.
Cover and bake one hour. Stir in cheese and cream, mixing thoroughly. Lower
temperature to 325 F and continue to bake 10 minutes longer.

This recipe can also be baked in a crock pot.

Serves 6

MOROCCAN CARROT SOUP

1 tbsp. olive oil
1 tsp. fennel seeds
1 1/2 lbs. (about 10 medium) carrots, sliced 1/4 inch thick
1/2 lb. sweet potatoes, peeled and cubed (about 2 medium)
1 large Granny Smith apple, peeled and diced
5 1/2 cups vegetable broth
1 tbsp. long grain white rice
1/2 tsp. curry powder
1/2 tsp. ground coriander
1 bay leaf
salt and freshly ground pepper to taste
fresh squeezed lemon juice to taste
fresh flat leaf parsley sprigs for garnish

In large pot heat oil over medium heat. Add fennel seeds and cook, stirring often, until fragrant (2 to 3 minutes). Add carrots, sweet potatoes and apple, and cook, stirring often, five minutes more. Add broth, rice, curry powder, coriander and bay leaf. Bring mixture to a boil and cover. Reduce heat and simmer until vegetables are tender, about 20 minutes. Discard bay leaf. Puree soup in batches in food processor, or with immersion blender. Add lemon juice, salt and freshly ground pepper to taste. Ladle soup into serving bowls and garnish with sprigs of parsley.

Serves 6
This soup is egg, dairy and meat free

SPANISH AVOCADO SOUP WITH GARLIC

2 tbsps. butter
1 medium onion, chopped
4 cups rich chicken stock
6 large garlic cloves, chopped
1 large avocado, ripe, peeled, seeded and chopped
juice of 1 lime
1 1/2 to 2 cups yogurt
salt and freshly ground pepper to taste

Saute' onion in the butter in large saucepan over medium heat until soft. Add stock and garlic and bring to simmer. Cover and cook 30 minutes. When slightly cooled, puree in batches in blender, and transfer to large bowl. Puree avocado and add to the transferred stock. Blend in yogurt and season with salt and pepper to taste.

Serve hot or cold garnished with minced green onion tops.
This soup can be kept for several days refrigerated, but may not be frozen for future use.

Serves 6

ONION AND CHEDDAR SOUP

4 onions, sliced coarsely
6 tbsps. butter
6 cups hot water
10 ozs. aged Cheddar cheese, grated
1/2 tbsp. Kikkoman soy sauce, or to taste
chopped pimientos for garnish

Simmer the onions in the butter in a heavy pot until golden brown. Put 4 cups hot water into a blender and add the onions and butter. Blend well and return to pot. Add 2 more cups hot water and the Cheddar cheese to the mixture, and mix well. Add the Kikkoman soy sauce, and heat to serving temperature. Garnish each serving with chopped pimientos.

Serves 6 to 8

POTAGE SAINT-GERMAIN

This soup is at its best when made with the very freshest fresh peas it is possible to obtain, but the following recipe is very, very delicious done with petit size frozen peas and the freshest Boston lettuce obtainable. See for yourself.

1/2 cup (1 stick) butter
1 small head Boston lettuce, cut into pieces
1 (12 oz.) package petit size frozen peas, or if you insist, 1 1/2 lbs. fresh peas, shelled
2 tsps. salt
1 tbsp. sugar
3 sprigs watercress (if unobtainable, chop 2 parsley sprigs, a very small diced onion, and about 1/2 cup finely chopped celery with leaves)
3 cups chicken stock, or broth

Melt the butter and cook the lettuce in it briefly along with the peas. Put lettuce and peas in a blender with the salt, sugar, watercress (or substituted other ingredients if using) and 1 cup of the chicken broth or stock, and blend until smooth. Return to the pan with remaining chicken broth or stock. Bring to a boil, turn heat down and simmer gently for 10 to 15 minutes.

Serves 4

SUMMER SQUASH SOUP

2 tbsps. butter or olive oil
2 onions, coarsely chopped (2 cups needed)
5 cups chicken broth or stock
2 potatoes, peeled and coarsely chopped (1 cup needed)
2 lbs. zucchini or yellow squash, or combination, coarsely chopped (8 cups needed)
2 carrots, sliced thin
salt to taste
fresh ground black pepper to taste
2 tbsps. fresh basil, finely chopped, or 1 tsp. dried
1 small lemon, juice only (or to taste), or 1 tbsp. dry white wine
squash blossoms, if available, for garnish

Melt butter or oil in a large saucepan over medium heat. Add onions and saute' until translucent, stirring constantly. Add broth and potatoes and bring to a boil, then cover and reduce heat to simmer. Simmer 5 minutes. Stir in carrots and sim-mer 8 to 10 more minutes, until potatoes and carrots are almost tender. Stir in squash, and seasonings. Simmer, covered, 10 to 15 minutes until vegetables are ten-der. Add lemon juice or wine to taste, and stir to mix. Serve either hot or cold. Garnish each serving with a fresh squash blossom if available.

Serves 6

TUSCAN BREAD SOUP

1 tbsp. olive oil
1/2 cup chopped onion
1/3 cup chopped celery
1/3 cup chopped carrot
1 garlic clove, minced
1 can (15 ozs.) white beans, rinsed
   and drained
1 3/4 cups. chicken broth

1 can (14 ozs.) tomatoes with
   juice
2 cups cabbage, chopped finely
1/4 cup diced red bell pepper
1/4 cup diced zucchini
1/8 tsp. thyme (or to taste)
4 slices toasted Italian bread
   cubed

Saute' the onion, celery, carrot and garlic in the olive oil. Add the beans, broth, tomatoes, cabbage, red bell pepper, zucchini and thyme and cook just until cabbage is tender. Put toasted cubes in four bowls and ladle soup on top and serve.

Serves 4 to 6

TUSCAN MINESTRONE

1 cup dried white beans
1/2 cup chick-peas
2 cups chopped yellow onions
4 cups peeled and cubed potatoes
1 cup coarsely chopped celery
2 tsps. finely chopped garlic
2 cups water or chicken or vegetable stock
1/3 cup virgin olive oil (ideally Tuscan or Chianti fresh green olive oil)
freshly ground white pepper to taste
1/2 pound spinach (stems discarded) coarsely shredded
Tuscan or other peasant style bread, thickly sliced
Freshly grated Parmesan cheese

Soak the dried beans and chick-peas in water for 8 hours, then pour into a large, heavy pot with a tight lid. Add water to 1 inch above the beans and peas. Bring to a boil, cover and cook over low heat until beans and peas are tender, about an hour. Add onions, potatoes, celery, garlic and water or broth plus the olive oil. Season with the freshly ground white pepper to taste. Add more water or broth as needed to bring liquid 1 to 2 inches above the vegetables. (Less liquid makes a thicker soup.) Bring soup to a boil and simmer uncovered until vegetables are crisp-tender. Remove from heat, and add the shredded spinach (should be about 4 cups lightly packed). Stir until spinach wilts.

To serve, use large soup bowls, place a slice of the bread in each, fill with soup, then sprinkle each serving with some of the freshly grated Parmesan cheese. Please note that it is very important that both the cheese and the white pepper be freshly grated.

Serves 6 - 8

FISH AND SEAFOOD SOUPS

BISQUES

A bisque is a puree of shellfish such as crawfish served as a soup. Early in the 19th century there were also bisques of pigeon and quail, but as time progressed the term gradually came to mean specifically shellfish purees. Such stylishly regarded soups are generally highly spiced.

LOBSTER BISQUE

This version of lobster bisque is typical of the spicy version of bisque, and much more the real thing than the many easier versions to be found.

Ingredients for a "mirepoix": 1/4 cup each finely julienned carrots, onions, celery, white of leek
4 tbsps. butter
2 tbsps. olive oil
1 lobster, live, 1 1/2 to 2 lbs.
1 cup white wine
1/4 cup cognac
1/2 cup uncooked rice

1 cup white wine
1/4 cup cognac
1/2 cup uncooked rice
4 cups fish stock or broth
salt and pepper to taste
1 cup heavy cream
2 tbsps. sherry
fresh parsley for garnish

In a heavy pot, make the mirepoix by sauteing the vegetables for 5 minutes in a mixture of 1 tbsp. of the butter and the 2 tbsps. of olive oil. Cut the lobster in half down the back, and cut crosswise into several pieces. Remove intestinal vein and add pieces to the pot. Move them about with two wooden spoons until the shells turn red. Add the wine and cognac, cover and simmer for 20 minutes. Remove from the heat, take the lobster meat out of the shell, and reserve. Break up the shells and either put through a food grinder, process in a food processor with steel blade, or pound in a mortar. Return the ground shells to the pot.

Cook the rice in 2 cups of the fish stock or broth for about 30 minutes, add to the ingredients in the pot, and puree in a food processor or put through a sieve.

Dilute the mixture with the remaining stock until the consistency of very thick soup is reached, and strain through a fine sieve. Season with salt and pepper to taste, reheat, adding the cream and remaining 3 tbsps. butter. Strain again, through a double thickness of cheesecloth.

At serving time, bring the soup to a simmer and add the sherry. Add a few cubes of lobster meat to each portion, reserving the rest for another use, and a sprinkling of the chopped parsley.

Serves 8

OYSTER BISQUE

1/2 cup uncooked rice
4 cups chicken broth
4 tbsps. butter
18 shucked oysters and their liquor

salt and freshly ground pepper
Tabasco sauce to taste
1 1/2 cups heavy cream
1/4 cup cognac

Cook the rice in the broth until very soft, then add the butter. Put rice through a sieve or whirl in a blender. Finely chop 12 of the oysters or whirl in a blender with their liquid. Add to the rice mixture. Season to taste with salt and pepper and dash or two of Tabasco. Stir in the heavy cream, heat just to the boiling point. Add the 6 whole oysters and heat just until they curl at the edges. Add the cognac and cook for 2 minutes. Ladle into heated soup cups, putting a whole oyster in each cup. Garnish with chopped parsley if desired.

Serves 6

OYSTER STEW

2 cups finely diced potatoes
1 cup water
1 pint oysters, drained and cut coarsely or chopped
1 pint oyster liquor (part clam broth or milk may be used)
1/3 cup butter
2 small onions finely diced
1/2 tbsp. Worcestershire sauce (Lea & Perrins preferred)
1/2 tsp. pepper
1 quart milk, plus 1 cup light cream or half and half
paprika to sprinkle on top of each bowl

Cook onions in butter until tender. Set aside. Cook potatoes in water at simmer until almost soft. Add reserved onions and butter. Stir to mix thoroughly. Add oysters and the 1 quart liquor with broth or milk if added to make the quart, and bring the mixture just to a boil. Remove from heat at once. Add cream and milk plus pepper and Worcestershire sauce. Just before serving heat completed stew but do not allow to boil. When hot, serve in individual bowls with a sprinkle of paprika on top.

Serves 6 to 8

BOUILLABAISSE

Bouillabaisse is a fish soup based on the historical version which originated in France in the general area of Marseilles long ago. In its many travels the types and number of fish as well, if any, (the original version said to have been without any wine of any kind entering into its preparation), the recipe itself has remained pretty much the same, but the kinds of fish involved and the wines involved now have changed in accordance with the different parts of the world in which it can be found. No matter which version is chosen it is important to remember that the bulk of the fish must be firm-fleshed, as the hard boil required of the dish will cause delicate fish to disintegrate, and that the hard boil itself is absolutely necessary for the coming together of the flavors.

3 lbs. filleted and skinned
    fish of firm white saltwater type
1 lb. filleted bass , or flounder
2 lbs heads, tails, bones and trim
    from the fish outlined above
2 quarts water
2 cups dry white wine
4 tbsps. butter
several leeks using both white and
    green parts, coarsely chopped
2 large stalks celery, strings
    removed and coarsely chopped
4 or 5 cloves garlic, coarsely chopped
2 medium large onions, chopped
1/2 cup fresh parsley, chopped
1/4 cup tomato paste
2 lb. 3 oz. can chopped tomatoes,
with juice

2 bay leaves, crumbled
1 tsp. dried thyme
1 tsp. fennel seed
grated rind of 1/2 fresh orange
2 tbsps. salt or to taste
white pepper to taste
1/2 cup olive oil
2 tbsps. light olive oil
3 dozen mussels or clams
2 lbs. lobster tails in the shells
2 1/2 tbsps. flour
Several splashes dry sherry
1/4 inch slices French bread
    dried in the oven to provide
    3 to 4 per person

Cut all the fish into slices or chunks roughly 2 by 3 inches. Keep the firm and delicate fish separate. (If you plan to marinate the fish, do this step the day before and follow directions for marinade in the note below.) Set aside.

Make the stock or base: Cut up the heads and bones in pieces and let them soak overnight in cold water to cover. Discard the soaking water and rinse well. Put heads and bones in a large, deep soup kettle and cover with the water and wine.

Melt the butter in a heavy skillet and add leeks, celery, garlic, onions and parsley. Cook, stirring, over moderate heat just until vegetables are softened, about 5 minutes.

Add to the stock kettle. (This step may be omitted and these vegetables added directly to the kettle without the brief saute'ing, but it adds to the depth of flavor and color to do so.)

Add the tomato paste, tomatoes, bay leaves, thyme, fennel seed, saffron, orange rind, salt and pepper. Pour the 1/2 cup olive oil over. Bring the liquid to a boil and cook hard for 8 minutes. Then cover, lower heat, and simmer for 40 minutes. While the stock is cooking, scrub the mussels and clams. With a heavy knife or kitchen shears cut the lobster tails into manageable pieces, cutting through shell and flesh. Set aside. Prepare a lie' to thicken the broth (stock): scoop out a half cup or so of the broth and put in a small, heavy saucepan. Stir in the flour and the remaining 2 1/2 tbsps. olive oil. Set over fairly high heat, bring to a boil, and cook for 3-5 minutes. Add to the kettle at the end of cooking time and stir in well.

Strain the broth through a strainer or large sieve placed over a bowl, pressing down on the vegetables and bones to extract all the juices. Return broth to the kettle. Bring broth again to a simmer and add the firm fish. Cook for 8 minutes over moderate heat, stirring frequently but gently with a wooden spoon. Add the tender fish, shellfish and lobster pieces and cook for 8 minutes more, using the spoon judiciously to bathe any exposed pieces with liquid but not hard enough to break up the fish. To serve, remove the fish, lobster and shellfish to one or two serving dishes and keep warm. Add the sherry to the broth and correct seasoning. Put bread slices in individual deep soup plates and moisten with a cupful or so of broth. Arrange a selection of fish and shellfish on top of each. Serve at once — bouillabaisse should not be kept waiting.

Note: To marinate the fish: Prepare the fish a day ahead. Moisten well with olive oil. In a small bowl make a mixture of 1 1/2 cups chopped tomatoes, 2 cloves garlic, pressed, 2 tbsps. coarse salt, freshly ground black pepper, a pinch of saffron, and 1 tsp. fennel powder. Sprinkle over fish. Cover and refrigerate overnight. Then proceed with the recipe, but season more cautiously than you would had you not used a marinade.

Serves 12

CIOPPINO

According to most culinary historians, the origin of California's most popular fish stew is of great interest to fans. Some feel it was originally Portuguese, while others that it is the work of transplanted Italian fishermen who probably introduced a fish stew known on the Ligurian coast of Italy as ciuppino, made with a variety of white fish and shellfish. The basic recipe is similar, and it is colored by the influence of the New World: crab makes its appearance, fish stock intensifies the flavor, and green pepper and mushrooms add their flavor notes as well. The wine, traditionally red, becomes an option.

Whatever the origin, fierce battles will probably continue to rage among cooks as to the best combination of fish for a cioppino, as well as between San Francisco and San Pedro, both of which claim to have originated the dish.

The following two recipes represent the modern versions of red and white wine cioppino.

SAN FRANCISCO RED WINE CIOPPINO

one 2 1/2 to 3 lb. bass (sea if possible) skinned and filleted
1 lb. raw shrimp, medium size
1 cooked Dungeness crab, fresh, or a 1 1/2 lb. lobster, cooked
18 littleneck clams in the shells, scrubbed
1 quart mussels, scrubbed and debearded
3 cups red wine
1/2 cup olive oil
1 large onion, chopped
3 tbsps. chopped fresh parsley
1/4 lb. mushrooms, sliced (do not use canned mushrooms)
1 green pepper, seeded
2 or 3 ripe tomatoes, peeled, seeded and coarsely chopped
3 ozs. tomato paste
salt and pepper to taste
1/2 tsp. cayenne pepper
1-2 tsps. dried basil (or 2 tbsps. fresh, finely chopped)

Cut the fish into serving pieces about 2 by 3 inches. Shell and devein the shrimp. Cut the crab into serving pieces or split and clean the lobster, crack the claws, and cut the body and tail into small serving pieces. Set aside whichever crustacean is being used.

Steam the clams and mussels in a deep pot with 1 cup of the wine until they open, discarding any which did not open. Remove from broth with a slotted spoon and reserve. Measure 1 cup of the broth, strain it through cheesecloth and reserve. (The broth may be murky at this point but will correct itself later.)

In a heavy, 7 quart soup pot, heat the olive oil and cook the onion, garlic, parsley, mushrooms and green pepper until the onions are translucent. Add the tomatoes and cook for 4 minutes. Add the strained broth, tomato paste, and remaining 2 cups of wine. Season with salt, pepper and cayenne, bring to a simmer, cover, lower flame to very gentle and simmer for about 20 minutes.

Add the basil and reserved fish, simmer for 8 to 10 minutes. Add the reserved shrimp, clams, mussels and crab or lobster and continue cooking at a gentle simmer, uncovered, until the shrimp are pink, about 5 minutes.

Serves 6 to 8

SAN PEDRO WHITE WINE CIOPPINO

2 tbsps. olive oil
2 tbsps. butter
3 cups chopped onions
2-4 cloves garlic, finely minced
2 green peppers, cored, seeded and chopped
4 cups peeled, seeded and chopped tomatoes
1 cup fresh or canned tomato sauce
1 tsp. dried basil
1 tsp. dried oregano
several dashes of cayenne pepper
salt and freshly ground pepper to taste
2 cups fresh fish stock*
2 cups dry white wine
1 lb. firm-fleshed fish (striped bass, red snapper, rock cod or sea bass)
    skinned and filleted and cut into bite-size pieces
1 lb. raw shrimp, shelled and deveined
1 dozen small clams, washed
1 lb. lobster tail cooked in the shell and cut into serving pieces
1 Dungeness crab, fresh or frozen, cooked in the shell and broken into
    pieces, or 3 6 1/2 oz. cans King crab meat, or 2 10 oz. pkgs.
    frozen crab meat

Heat the oil and butter in a large, heavy kettle and add the onions and garlic. Cook,
stirring often, until the garlic is lightly colored. Add the green peppers and continue
cooking and stirring until the peppers wilt. Add the tomatoes, tomato sauce, basil
oregano and cayenne, salt and pepper to taste. Add the fish stock and cook slowly
for about 2 hours, stirring often to prevent burning. More fish stock may be added
if needed. Add the wine and continue cooking for about 10 minutes. (The soup
may be made ahead to this point.) About 20 minutes before serving, return soup to
a boil, add the fish and cook for about 5 minutes. Add the shrimp, simmer for about
8 minutes, then add the clams, lobster tail and crab. Cook, stirring gently, for about
5 minutes (or until the clams open). Serve in very hot soup bowls with garlic bread.

Serves 10

*See recipe for fish fumet or stock in section on Stocks herein

48

FRESH SALMON CHOWDER

This recipe may be made with salmon collars, which are the neck portions of the fresh salmon which the fish market cuts off when the fish is cut into steaks. Ask your market to reserve these for you or to save small pieces left when the steaks are cut. This is a great dish and saves a great deal of otherwise wasted salmon.

2 lbs. salmon
1 cup water
1 small onion, finely chopped
2 tbsps. butter
2 cups potatoes, peeled and cut into 1/2 inch cubes

Boil the salmon pieces in the water until just done (do not overcook), drain and skim the liquid, and remove the bones, skin and dark parts from the fish. Fry the onion in the butter only until clear (do not brown). Parboil the potatoes in enough water to cover for 5 minutes and drain. Add the potatoes and fish liquid to the cooked onions.

Grind in a mortar the following:

1 tsp. salt
1 tsp. herb salt*
1/8 tsp. fish herbs blend*
1/8 tsp. white pepper

Add herb mixture to potato and onion mixture and cook for 5 minutes, then cover and simmer about 10 minutes, then add the following:

1 cup coffee cream
1 cup scalded milk
5 soda crackers, soaked in a little of the milk
2 tbsps. butter
the cooked salmon

Do not boil, but serve very hot. Too much heating may curdle the soup. If this happens, drain off liquid and put it through a blender and then mix with the solids and reheat.

* These may be found in the Glossary section of this book.

Serves 6

MANHATTAN STYLE CLAM CHOWDER

1 quart chowder clams (or 4 10 1/2 oz. cans minced clams) with their
    liquid.
1/2 lb. bacon, cut into 1/4 inch pieces
3 medium onions, finely chopped
1 small green pepper, finely chopped
2 cups peeled, seeded and chopped tomatoes, or 1 lb. 12 oz. can chopped
    tomatoes, juice reserved.
3 medium potatoes, diced
4 carrots, diced
2 stalks celery, diced
1 1/2 quarts water
salt and freshly ground black pepper to taste
1 tsp. dried thyme
1 bay leaf

Drain off the clam liquid and reserve. Chop the clams finely (unless using the canned minced clams) and set aside. Cook the bacon in a heavy pan until almost crisp, remove with slotted spoon and reserve. Add onions and green pepper to the hot bacon fat and saute' until onions are pale gold. Remove to large cooking pot and add tomatoes and their juice, potatoes, carrots, celery and 1 1/2 quarts water. Season with salt if necessary, remembering that clams can be salty, and pepper to taste. Add thyme and bay leaf and bring to a boil. Lower the heat and simmer gently, uncovered, for about 40 minutes, or until the potatoes are tender. Add the clams and their juice, cover and simmer for 20 minutes longer. Correct the seasonings if necessary and add the reserved bacon. Serve hot but do not allow soup to boil.

Serves 6

NEW ENGLAND CLAM CHOWDER

4 tbsps. butter
5 tbsps. flour
4 cups milk
1 13 oz. can evaporated milk (reserve can and add 1 can water)
1 oz. salt pork, rind removed and cut into small cubes
1 small onion, finely chopped
2 small potatoes (peeled and coarsely chopped, and boiled in a small amount of
   water until tender)
1 tsp. fresh pressed garlic (or to taste)
2 tsps. grated onion
1/4 tsp. basil
1/4 tsp. marjoram
1 1/2 pints minced clams with their juice
salt and pepper to taste

Melt butter in saucepan and add flour. Blend in the milk, evaporated milk, and water, and cook until thickened. Fry the pork until crisp, but not brown. Add the onion and cook until soft. Mix all ingredients together, add the seasonings and salt and pepper to taste and the clams with their juice. Heat over (not in) hot water to serving temperature only. Do not allow to get very hot or boil after clams have been added as soup may tend to curdle if it gets too hot. Garnish with a little paprika on top of each bowl when served.

Serves 8

SERIOUS SEA SCALLOP SOUP

3 cups scallops (much preferred are sea scallops if possible)
1 tbsp. freshly squeezed lemon juice
3 tbsps. butter
1 cup water
1 quart milk
salt to taste
1 tsp. paprika
sliced lime

Chop the scallops coarsely and sprinkle with the lemon juice. Allow to stand for about 20 minutes, stirring gently once or twice. Add 1 cup water and bring to a boil in medium pot. Add the butter, salt to taste, paprika and milk. Cook for about 8 minutes. Serve in small bowls with a slice of lime in each.

Serves 4 to 6

SHRIMP GUMBO

1/4 cup flour
4 tbsps. bacon drippings
16 ozs. clam juice (two 8 oz. bottles)
1 large can Italian plum tomatoes, drained
2 bay leaves
2 tsps. Worcestershire sauce (Lea & Perrins brand a must)
1/4 tsp. thyme
salt to taste
1 tsp. sugar
freshly ground black pepper to taste
2 lbs. raw shrimp, peeled and deveined, small to medium size
1 pkg. frozen okra
1 tsp. grated lemon peel
1/2 tsp. file' powder
chopped parsley
hot cooked rice.

Brown the flour in a dry skillet, stirring. Cook the onions in the bacon drippings in a deep pot until the onion becomes translucent, about 5 minutes. Sprinkle the browned flour over the onion mixture and stir in the clam juice. Cook over low heat, stirring constantly, until smooth and thickened. Add the tomatoes, bay leaf, Lea & Perrins, seasonings (except for the file' powder) and shrimp. Cook for about 10 minutes or until the shrimp begin to curl, add the frozen okra and stir until the pieces are separated. Cook until okra is tender but still crisp. Remove from the heat, add the file' powder and transfer to a tureen. Serve in soup bowls in each of which a large spoonful of hot, cooked rice has been placed. Sprinkle chopped parsley on top. Do not allow the file' powder to be cooked, so be sure to add it at the last minute.

Serves 4 to 6

FOWL SOUPS

BETTER THAN MOM'S

4 whole bone-in chicken legs
4 cups chicken broth
2 cups water
5 cloves garlic, minced
2 tbsps. chopped fresh ginger
1/4 tsp. black pepper
3 carrots, sliced
1 lg. leek, white part and some of the green, rinsed, cut into 1/2" slices
1 lg. sweet potato, peeled and cut into large chunks
6 cups packed, torn spinach; or 1/2 package frozen
1 lg. tomato cut into 1/2" chunks
1/4 to 1 tsp. hot-pepper sauce

Divide the chicken legs into thigh and drumstick portions. Discard the skin and visible fat. Place chicken in large saucepan or Dutch oven. Add broth, water, garlic, ginger and pepper. Bring to a boil over high heat, skimming off any foam that rises to the surface. Reduce the heat to low, cover, and simmer for 15 minutes, skimming the surface occasionally.

Stir in the carrots, leek, and sweet potato. Cover, and simmer for 20 minutes, or until vegetables are tender and chicken is cooked through.

Add spinach and tomato, and cook for five minutes, or until spinach is wilted and tomato is heated through. Add the hot-pepper sauce gradually, to taste.

Serves 4

CHICKEN AND CORN CHOWDER WITH THYME

6 slices bacon, diced
4 green onions, chopped, for garnish
1 onion, chopped
2 (14 oz.) cans chicken broth; or 4 cups home made
2 large potatoes, diced
4 cups frozen corn kernels
4 skinless, boneless chicken breast halves; cut into cubes
3 tbsps. fresh thyme, chopped
2 cups half-and-half
Salt and pepper to taste

In a large pot, cook bacon until crisp. Remove, drain, set aside. Drain all but 3 tbsps.. bacon fat from the pan.

Sauté the onion in the bacon fat. Add broth and potatoes to the pot. Cover, and simmer for 10 minutes.

Add corn, chicken and thyme. Simmer until chicken is cooked and vegetables are tender, about 15 minutes. Stir half-and-half into the soup, and simmer for two minutes. Ladle into bowls, and sprinkle with bacon and green onions.

Serves 6

CHICKEN PASTA SOUP

4 to 6 boneless, skinless chicken breasts cut into slices
1/2 tsp. seasoned salt
4 tbsps. olive oil
1/2 cup butter, divided
1 small onion, diced
2 stalks celery, sliced thin
1 carrot, peeled and shredded
1/2 cup flour
2 cans (14 oz.) (or 4 cups home made) chicken broth
cayenne and black pepper
1/4 tsp. basil
2 cups light cream
4 oz. fresh mushrooms, sliced
1 cup sugar snap peas
1 tbsp. sugar, optional
6 to 8 oz. penne pasta, cooked and drained

Season the chicken with seasoned salt; sauté in a large heavy saucepan in olive oil until lightly browned. Remove chicken. Add 2 tbsps. butter to the pan, and sauté onion, celery, and carrot until soft. Stir in flour and gradually add chicken broth. Add the sliced chicken, peppers, and basil. Stir in the cream, and heat on low.

Melt the remaining 2 tbsps. butter in another pan, and cook mushrooms, pea pods and sugar for five minutes. Combine with first pan, and simmer 10 minutes. Add the cooked pasta and serve.

SOPA DE TORTILLA

This recipe is from the old Salmagundi Restaurant in San Francisco.

3 lbs. chicken pieces
4 qts. water
1 tsp. celery seeds
1 tsp. whole black peppercorns
2 cloves garlic, peeled
1 (1 lb.) can whole, peeled
  tomatoes, undrained
1 onion, chopped into one
  inch pieces
1 green pepper, cut into one
  inch squares
3 sprigs fresh cilantro

1/2 tsp. ground cumin
1/4 tsp. cayenne pepper
1/4 tsp. freshly ground pepper
1 clove garlic, minced
1 (10 oz.) pkg. frozen corn
4 green onions, chopped
salt to taste
1 cup cooked rice
2 tsps. minced fresh parsley
tortilla chips and freshly
  grated cheddar cheese for garnish

Combine chicken and water in stockpot. Add celery seeds, peppercorns and garlic tied in small cheesecloth square. Cover and bring to a boil, then reduce heat and simmer until chicken is tender, about 45 minutes. Remove chicken from broth and let cool. Strain broth and return to stockpot. Add next 8 ingredients, cover and simmer 30 minutes. Add corn and green onion and simmer 10 minutes more. Season with salt to taste. When chicken is cool enough to manage, skin and bone it and dice meat into 1 inch pieces. Add to the broth with rice and parsley and heat through. Ladle into warm bowls and garnish with tortilla chips and cheddar cheese.

Serves 6 to 8

VEGETABLE TURKEY SOUP

2 medium onions, chopped
2 tbsps. olive oil
1/2 lb. ground turkey
2 cloves garlic, minced
3 cups chicken broth
1 28-oz. can chopped tomatoes with juice
1 cup diced potatoes
1 cup sliced celery
1 cup sliced carrots
1 cup sliced mushrooms
1/2 cup chopped fresh parsley
1 cup. green peas, fresh or frozen
1 cup dry white or rose' wine

Sauté onions in oil in a heavy soup pot, until tender. Add ground turkey and garlic, separating turkey with a fork, until brown. Add remaining ingredients, except peas and wine, bring to a boil, and simmer gently about 1 hour. Add peas and wine and simmer gently another 10 to 15 minutes. Adjust seasonings and serve.

Serves 8

VIETNAMESE CHICKEN SOUP

5 lbs. chicken necks, backs, wings
4 cups water
1 cup cooked rice
1 cup flaked crab meat
1 tsp. cilantro
1 chicken bouillon cube
salt to taste

Prepare a rich broth by simmering the 5 lbs. chicken bones in the 4 cups water for 1 1/2 hours. Strain, skim and reserve broth and the meat from the chicken. Mix together the rice, crab meat, cilantro, bouillon cube and dash salt to taste, with the broth and chicken just cooked. Heat to serving temperature, testing for taste, and adding a little water to the broth if needed. Garnish each serving with fresh, chopped cilantro.

Serves 4 to 6

WHITE CHICKEN CHILI

1 cup chopped onion
3 cloves of garlic, minced
6 tbsps. butter
1 tbsp. chili powder
2 tsps. ground cumin
1 tsp. cayenne pepper
6 tbsps. flour
3 cups chicken broth
3 lbs. skinless chicken breasts, cubed
2 cans (15 oz.) cannelloni beans, drained
1 cup plain yogurt, low fat if preferred

Toppings: chopped red onion, chopped cilantro, grated cheese

Sauté onion and garlic in butter. Add spices and flour and cook 2 to 3 minutes, stirring constantly. Stir in the broth slowly, bringing to a boil. Add chicken and cook 2 minutes. Add beans and yogurt, stirring just until heated through. Season with salt and pepper to taste.. Serve with optional toppings.

Serves 8

MEAT AND VEGETABLE SOUPS

OLD FASHIONED BEEF AND VEGETABLE STEW

This recipe is a contribution by the well known Chef Greg Atkinson, who recommends using naturally raised beef and organic vegetables. We will leave it to you to choose.

1/4 cup olive oil
2 tbsps. butter
6 tbsps. flour
1 lb. beef stew meat, cut into 1 inch chunks
2 cups celery, sliced
2 cups carrots, peeled and sliced
1 medium onion, peeled and chopped coarsely
4 cups beef broth
2 tbsps. finely chopped garlic
2 tsps.kosher salt, or to taste
1 tsp. freshly ground pepper
1 lb. red potatoes, cut into 1 inch cubes
2 cups (about 1/4 lb.) sliced mushrooms
1 1/2 cups frozen sweet peas
1/4 cup fresh parsley, finely chopped

Heat olive oil and butter in a very large pot over medium high heat, stirring until melted and hot. Stir in flour and continue stirring the roux until the foam subsides and the mixture is uniformly nut brown in color. This will take about 5 minutes. Stir the beef into the roux and brown on all sides about 5 minutes. Stir in the carrots, celery and onion and cook for 1 or 2 minutes longer. Add beef broth and garlic and cook over medium heat, stirring often, for about 45 minutes. Add the potatoes and continue cooking until tender, about 30 minutes. Add mushrooms. When the mushrooms have taken up enough broth to sink into the stew, turn off the heat. Stir in the parsley and peas, and when heated through the stew is ready to serve.

Serves 4

BEEFY FRENCH ONION SOUP

The traditional onion soup of the Paris market, Les Halles, is a rich beef broth, dense with onions and crowned with a huge pile of cheese atop a big piece of toast. It is so filling that it is almost a meal. This recipe takes the soup yet a richer step by making the broth from meaty beef shanks. All else needed is a leafy green salad and a robust red wine. The broth can be prepared, of course, a day or so in advance.

3 1/2 to 4 lbs. beef shanks
6 tbsps. butter
1 tbsp. olive oil
1 large onion, finely chopped
2 large carrots, thinly sliced
1 tbsp. salt
1/2 tbsp. whole black peppers
5 sprigs fresh parsley
1 bay leaf
2 qts. water
8 medium onions, thinly sliced and separated into rings
1 or 2 cloves garlic, minced or pressed
2 tbsps. flour
1 cup dry white wine
6 thick slices French bread
1 cup each shredded Swiss and Parmesan cheese

In a large soup kettle (6 qts. or more) brown beef shanks well on all sides in 1 tbsp. butter and oil. Add chopped onion, carrots, salt, black peppers, parsley, bay leaf and water. Bring to boiling, reduce heat, cover and simmer for about 3 hours, until broth is richly flavored. Strain broth into a large bowl. When meat is cool enough to handle, return it and the marrow from the bones to the broth in chunks, discarding vegetables and bones. Chill soup and skim off the fat (can be done 1 or 2 days ahead). In the same kettle, heat remaining 5 tbsps. butter. Add sliced onions, cover and cook until limp (about 10 minutes). Uncover and cook over low heat, stirring frequently, until onions brown lightly, about 30 minutes more. Reduce heat if onions begin to become too brown too fast. Stir in garlic and flour. Cook and stir until bubbly. Remove from heat and stir in about 1 qt. of the broth. Return to heat and mix in remaining broth with beef and wine. Bring to a gentle boil, cover, reduce heat and simmer until ready to serve. Taste for salt.
Now, place bread in single layer on baking sheet in a 250 F. oven. Toast for about 30 minutes, until bread is very dry and barely browned. Sprinkle about 1/3 cup mixed cheeses over each piece. To serve, ladle soup into bowls, top each with cheese topped toast, and place under broiler for about 3 minutes about 5 inches from heat. Serve at once.

Serves 6

BLACK BEAN AND HAM SOUP

1/2 lb. black beans
2 tbsps. butter
1 celery stalk, chopped
1/2 cup onions, chopped
2 tsps. flour
1 bay leaf

1 ham bone with rind, plus ham pieces
1/4 cup fresh parsley chopped
freshly ground pepper to taste
1 cup dry white wine
1 tbsp. cider vinegar
1/2 cup sour cream

Wash beans, cover with water and let stand overnight. Drain. Add water to cover and simmer about 2 hours. Saute' celery and onions in butter until soft. Add flour, cook and stir until thickened. Stir into beans along with bay leaf, ham bone, parsley and pepper. Simmer about 2 hours. Remove ham bone, trimming any meat to return to soup, and add ham pieces. Puree soup in blender, or mash. Add wine and vinegar and heat until hot. Add sour cream to the soup to serve, or serve as a topping.

Serves 4 to 6

UKRAINIAN BORSCHT

This version of Borscht uses sausage along with the beef, and the better the sausage the better the soup. Polish kielbasa has a rich flavor, but Canadian bacon can be used, also frankfurters, chipolatas or either the sweet or hot Italian sausage. Italian sausages should be sauteed slightly, before they are added to the soup, to get rid of the excess fat.

2 lbs. soup beef with cracked bone
1 lb. lean fresh pork
1/2 lb. smoked pork
1 bay leaf
10 peppercorns
1 clove garlic, crushed
few sprigs parsley
1 carrot, sliced
1 stalk celery, sliced
1 leek, sliced
1 (1 lb.14 oz.) can beets or
   8 medium beets

1/2 green cabbage, chopped
2 large tomatoes, peeled and
   quartered
2 large onions, quartered
2 tsps. sugar
2 tbsps. vinegar
1/2 cup cooked or canned navy
   beans
1 kielbasa (Polish) sausage or
5 frankfurters, sliced thick
salt to taste

Put the beef, bone and 2 1/2 quarts of water in a kettle. Cover and bring to a boil. Simmer for 1 hour. Add the pork, bay leaf, peppercorns, garlic, parsley, carrot, celery and leek. Cover and bring to a boil. Simmer for 2 hours. If using fresh beets, put the beets except for one in a pan with boiling water to cover. Simmer, covered, for 1 hour. Peel and cut into eighths. Remove all the meat from the pot and save. Strain the broth and discard the tired vegetables. Skim off the excess fat. (This is easily done if the broth is refrigerated overnight.) Return the broth to the kettle with the cooked fresh beets or the canned ones with their juice, kielbasa, if used, cabbage, tomatoes, onions, vinegar and sugar. Cover and cook for 30 minutes. Add the beans and frankfurters (if using). Cook for 10 minutes. Slice whichever meat is being used, and add to the soup with the one raw beet, peeled and grated, unless you have used canned beets, in which case omit this step.

Serves 10 to 12 lavishly.

BURT'S BEEF STEW

Here is a recipe purported to be a favorite of Burt Reynolds!

3 slices bacon, cut into small pieces
4 tbsps. flour
1/4 tsp. freshly ground pepper
2 lbs. lean beef, cut in chunks
1 large onion, chopped
2 cloves garlic, minced
1 can (28 oz.) tomato sauce
1 cup beef broth
1 cup dry red wine
1 bay leaf
1/2 tsp. thyme
3 carrots, cut up coarsely
2 stalks celery, cut up coarsely
4 large potatoes, peeled and cut into quarters
10 or 12 fresh mushrooms, sliced

Cook bacon until brown in a large pot or Dutch oven. Dip beef in a mixture of flour and pepper and brown in the bacon fat, turning often. (Add a little olive oil if needed.) Add onion and garlic and brown them slightly. Add tomato sauce, broth, wine, bay leaf and thyme. Cover and cook slowly for about 1 1/2 hours. Add carrots, celery, then potatoes and mushrooms. Cover and cook until vegetables are tender (about 30 minutes more).

Variation: Add a package of frozen mixed vegetables and serve over baked potatoes.

Serves 6 to 8

CHINESE WATERCRESS SOUP

This is a "different" Oriental soup, and takes a little time to put together, but makes a very tasty, interesting light meal, with toast or flatbread, in itself.

6 cups chicken broth, without fat
soy sauce to taste
2 large bunches watercress,
   washed and trimmed

4 poached eggs
4 tbsps. finely diced water
   chestnuts
12 thin strips Virginia ham

Heat the chicken broth to boiling, season to taste with soy sauce. Arrange watercress in the bottom of a tureen, like a nest, and carefully lower the poached eggs onto it. Sprinkle with the water chestnuts and ham. Very carefully pour the boiling broth down the side of the tureen, so as not to upset the watercress and eggs on the bottom. Serve each person an egg and some cress, water chestnuts, ham and broth. The tureen needs to be hot before beginning, and the broth boiling, the watercress crisp and the eggs poached to firm. Serve with some thin crisp flatbread, or thin toast.

Serves 4

CORN CHOWDER WITH BACON

This is a contribution to our book given us by the well known master chef Greg Atkinson, which we believe you will find unusual and different, plus delicious.

4 cups milk
2 cups chicken or vegetable broth
4 medium Yukon Gold potatoes (about 2 lbs.) scrubbed and diced
1/4 pound bacon, cut into bits
1 medium onion, finely diced
2 stalks celery, finely diced
6 cloves garlic, minced or pressed
1 tsp. fresh thyme or 1/2 tsp. dried
2 tbsps. flour
6 ears of fresh corn, husked
2 tsps. kosher salt (or to taste)
1 tsp. freshly ground pepper
chopped fresh parsley

Put the milk and broth into a large soup pot over medium high heat and bring to a boil. Add the potatoes to the milk mixture and cover. Reduce the heat to simmer and cook until very tender, about 15 minutes. Cook bacon and remove, saving fat. Saute' the onion and celery in the fat until soft. Stir in the garlic and thyme, then the flour. Add a ladle of the milk mixture to the sauted vegetables and stir, then add a second ladle. Transfer the vegetable mixture to the soup pot. Scrape the kernels from the corn ears and stir into the soup. Simmer gently until the corn is tender, about 10 minutes. Season to taste.
Serve hot with bacon bits and chopped parsley on top. Vegetarians may skip the bacon and use 3 tbsps. butter instead.

Serves 8

CURRIED LENTIL, TOMATO AND LAMB STEW

1 tsp. olive oil
1 lb. trimmed boneless lamb sirloin, cut into 1 inch pieces
1 1/2 cups chopped onion
4 garlic cloves, minced
1 tsp. minced, peeled ginger
1 1/2 tbsps. curry powder
2 tsps. garam masala
2 cups water
1 1/2 cups canned diced tomatoes in their juice
1 cup dried green or brown lentils
3 carrots, peeled and thickly sliced
1 cup frozen green peas

Heat oil in heavy large pot over medium high heat. Sprinkle lamb with salt and pepper. Add to the pot. Saute' until brown, about 5 minutes. Add curry powder and stir 30 seconds. Add 2 cups water and next 3 ingredients. Bring to a boil, and reduce heat. Cover and simmer until lamb and lentils are tender, stirring occasionally, about 1 hour.
Add peas to the pot and simmer until heated through, about 5 minutes. Season with salt and pepper. Ladle into bowls.

Serves 4

CURRIED PUMPKIN SOUP

For a dramatic presentation, serve this succulent and spice rich soup in the shell.

One 7 to 8 lb. pumpkin, or 4 cups pumpkin puree
6 cups homemade chicken stock, or 3 (14 1/2 oz.) cans chicken broth
2 large tart apples, peeled, cored and chopped
1 carrot, chopped
2 tsps. grated ginger root
1 tsp. curry powder, or to taste
1/2 tsp. ground cumin
6 slices bacon
1/4 cup chopped onion
2 tbsps. sugar
1 cup croutons

With large, sharp knife, slice off top fourth of the pumpkin and set aside. Scoop out seeds and stringy pulp. Replace top. Place pumpkin on a 15x10x1 inch baking pan. Bake in a 375 F oven for 50 to 60 minutes or until pumpkin flesh can be scooped out easily. Cool slightly, scoop out and reserve pumpkin flesh, leaving flesh on bottom of shell and leaving about a 3/4 inch thickness on walls. Cut into chunks (you should have about 4 cups).

In a large pot, combine 4 cups pumpkin, broth, apple, carrot, ginger root, curry powder and cumin. Bring to boiling, then reduce heat. Cover and simmer for 10 to 12 minutes or until vegetables are tender. Cool slightly and process in small batches in blender. Place shell in a large casserole and pour soup into the shell. Bake, covered, in a 375 F oven for 20 minutes.

Meanwhile, cook bacon in a skillet until crisp. Drain, reserving 1 tbsp. drippings. Cook onion and sugar in drippings until tender. Crumble the bacon, stir it with the croutons into skillet. Sprinkle mixture on top of soup in pumpkin. Ladle the soup into bowls and serve.

Makes 6 to 8 servings

EASY EGGPLANT SOUP

This is a great recipe for a short notice meal. From start to finish it is ready to serve in less than an hour and along with a bread makes a hearty, whole dinner.

1 lb. ground beef, crumbled
1 large onion, chopped
1 tbsp. each butter and olive oil
1 or 2 large cloves garlic, minced or pressed
1 medium eggplant (about 1 1/2 lbs.) cut into 3/4 inch cubes, unpeeled
2 medium carrots, shredded
1 green pepper, seeded and cut into 2 inch strips
1 large can (28 oz.) chopped tomatoes
1 tsp. each salt, sugar and dried basil
1/2 tsp. ground nutmeg
1/4 tsp. freshly ground pepper
2 cans (13 3/4 oz. each) regular strength beef broth, or 3 1/2 cups
     homemade beef broth
1/2 cup chopped fresh parsley
freshly shredded Parmesan cheese

Brown beef and onion in butter and oil in a 5 to 6 quart Dutch oven. Add garlic, eggplant, carrots and green pepper and cook, stirring occasionally, until eggplant browns lightly. Stir in tomatoes and their liquid, salt, sugar, basil, nutmeg, pepper and broth. Bring to a boil, reduce heat, cover and simmer for 45 to 50 minutes, or until the eggplant is very tender.

Stir in parsley and salt to taste. Serve with cheese at the table.

Serves 4 to 6

HOLIDAY BAZAAR COUNTRY BEAN SOUP

The crafts group at the San Juan Island Mullis Senior Center in Friday Harbor sells these colorful beans in small containers along with this recipe during the annual Christmas Holiday bazaars:

2 cups mixed variety of dry beans (the more colorful the better)
2 qts. water
2 lbs. chopped baked ham, divided into two portions, or a meaty
   ham hock
1 onion, finely chopped
2 cloves garlic, minced
   freshly ground pepper to taste
1 14 oz. can chopped tomatoes with juice
1   10 oz. can tomatoes with green chilies with juice
4 carrots, sliced 1/2 inch thick
2 stalks celery, chopped

Rinse the beans and soak overnight in water. Drain the beans and put into a pot with 2 quarts fresh water. Add half the ham or the ham hock, the onion, garlic, and the freshly ground pepper. Bring to a boil, reduce heat, cover and simmer 2 to 2/12 hours or until the beans are tender. Add the tomatoes, carrots and celery and simmer an additional 30 minutes. Add the second half of the ham (or remove the meat from the ham hock and return the meat to the pot) and heat before serving. Chicken or beef may be substituted for the ham, merely adjusting the seasonings to taste.

Serves 6 to 8

JUNE MULLIS' HEARTY LENTIL SOUP

3/4 cup lentils, soaked overnight
3 medium carrots, sliced
1/2 cup onions, finely chopped
1/4 cup celery leaves, chopped
1 tbsp. fresh basil, chopped or 1 tsp. dried
1 large bay leaf
1 tsp. dried oregano
1/4 lb. baked ham, diced
1 qt. chicken or beef broth
1 lb. lean ground round
salt and pepper to taste

Chop all vegetables. Combine them with seasonings in a large bowl. Add the ham. In a large pot bring broth to a light boil. Drop ground round into the broth in small bits, about the size of a sugar cube. Drain the lentils and add them to the pot with the vegetables, seasonings and ham. Bring to a boil and reduce heat. Simmer light- ly for two hours, adding water as needed. Remove bay leaf before serving.

Serves 6 to 8

LAMB SHANK STEW

1 large lamb shank, washed and trimmed
water or chicken broth to cover
1 tsp. each pepper and Italian style herbs
1 medium sweet onion cut into 1/2 inch squares
2 large cloves garlic, minced or put through a press
2 tbsps. olive oil
1 lb. green beans, trimmed and cut into 2 to 3 inch pieces
1 can (14 oz.) plum tomatoes with puree, or use fresh tomatoes plus
  their juice
salt, pepper and ground cloves to taste
steamed rice for 2

Place lamb shank and liquid in a large pot and bring to a boil. Reduce heat and simmer for about 3 hours, skimming off any foam, or use a slow cooker for this step. Cover during cooking process, and continue to cook until tender. Remove the meat from the pot. Skim the fat off and sieve the broth. Remove the meat from the bones and cut into bite sized chunks. Return the broth to the pot and set aside the meat. In a large skillet brown onion and garlic in olive oil. Add beans and gently saute' all together for about 5 minutes, then add the onion mixture to the pot and cook, covered, until the beans are tender (about 15 to 20 minutes). Add the meat, tomatoes and seasonings (adjusting seasonings to taste), and cook another 3 minutes or so until all ingredients are hot and thoroughly mixed.
Serve over steamed white rice.

Serves 2 generously

MARY JANE'S ZUCCHINI SOUP

1 lb. hamburger
5 medium zucchini, cut in large cubes
2 cups chopped celery
2 cups chopped green pepper
1/2 medium cabbage, grated
2 cans (4 ozs. ea.) mushrooms or equivalent fresh
8 bouillon cubes dissolved in
6 cups boiling water
1 can (46 ozs.) tomato juice, or 2 large cans (28ozs.) tomatoes
1 large onion, chopped
1 tbsp. oregano (or less to taste)
1/2 tsp. basil
1 large garlic clove, minced or pressed
salt and pepper to taste

Saute' hamburger in a little olive oil in a big pot until lightly browned. Add all other ingredients and bring to simmer. Cover and continue to simmer, gently, stirring often,for about 2 hours more.

Serves 6 to 8

MINESTRONE WITH SAUSAGE SOUP

1 1/2 mild Italian sausage rings with casing removed and sliced
2 cloves garlic, minced
2 medium onions, minced
1 can (28 ozs.) chopped Italian tomatoes
4 cups beef broth
1 1/4 cups water
1 1/2 cups dry red wine
1/2 tsp. basil
1/4 to 1/2 cup chopped celery
1 green pepper, chopped
2 medium zucchini, sliced
1 1/2 cups cooked small pasta shells
1/4 cup chopped parsley
1/4 cup Parmesan cheese, grated

Saute' sausage until cooked. Pour off fat and add garlic, onion and tomatoes. Add broth, water, red wine, basil and remaining ingredients except cheese. Simmer covered for 45 minutes to 1 hour until vegetables are tender. Serve with grated cheese on top.

Serves 6 to 8

OZARK MOUNTAINS WINTER VEGETABLE SOUP

This is a wonderfully satisfying meat and vegetable soup which my mother used to make during my childhood years, learned from her mother, and now enjoyed by all my children and their children. It recalls the past with its long, cold winter nights in the mountains with its soothing and filling warmth. Here, of course, it is presented with a modern set of equipment.

1 lb. beef soup bones
1 lb. beef shank slice, browned in oil in a skillet
3 cups water
1 can (14.5 oz.) diced tomatoes
1 can (8 oz.) tomato sauce
1 onion, chopped coarsely
1 tbsp. Lea & Perrins Worcestershire Sauce (no other will do for me)
2 carrots, peeled and chopped coarsely
2 potatoes, peeled and chopped coarsely
1/2 small head of cabbage, chopped coarsely
1 1/2 tsps. sugar (or sugar substitute)
1 can (8 oz.) cream style corn

Put beef meat and bones, water, 2 tomato products and onion in a 6 quart slow cooker. Cook on low for 4 to 6 hours. Add Lea & Perrins, carrots, potatoes, cabbage and sugar or sweetener and cook on high for 2 to 3 hours more until tender. Add cream of corn at the very last only until hot.

This recipe may also be made in a pressure cooker, giving 20 minutes to pressurize the meat and bones in the water, a cooling period to enable removal of the meat and marrow from the bones, then 5 minutes for the final pressurized cooking of meat, marrow and the vegetables (except the corn). Add the corn after pressure is back down and dish is ready to serve.

Prepared by either method, served with toasted sourdough bread slices sprinkled with butter and Parmesan cheese equals delicious!

Serves 6

PORTUGUESE SOUP

This hearty sausage and vegetable soup will feed a hungry group of people on a cold winter day. Great for feeding a large family.

2 cups onion, chopped
3 large cloves garlic, minced or pressed
2 tbsps. rich olive oil
1 lb. pork or beef, garlic flavored, Polish sausage
12 small new potatoes, quartered
10 cups beef broth
1 small head cabbage, chopped
2 (16 oz.) cans pinto beans
1/2 cup cider vinegar
1 (16 oz.) bottle catsup

Saute' onions and garlic in the oil. When transparent, add sausage which has been thickly sliced. Brown sausage slightly and add all other ingredients. Simmer, covered, 30 to 45 minutes on low, stirring occasionally. Serve very hot. This soup will keep for three or four days refrigerated, but does not freeze well. Makes 4 to 5 quarts.

Serves 8 or more

RED LENTIL SOUP WITH SMOKED HAM OR TURKEY

2 tbsps. butter
1 onion, chopped
1 celery stalk, chopped
1 medium carrot, chopped
1 leek, white part only, chopped
8 medium white mushrooms,
    quartered
1/2 cup dry white wine
5 cups chicken stock

1 cup water
2 tbsps. dried thyme, ground
2 bay leaves
1 cup dried red lentils
8 ozs. smoked ham, turkey or
    chicken, diced
salt and pepper to taste

Melt butter in pan and saute' onion, celery,carrots and mushrooms until golden, (about 3 or 4 minutes). Stir in wine, stock and water and bring to boil. Add thyme and bay leaf. Lower heat, cover and simmer gently 20 minutes. Add lentils and continue cooking, covered, until lentils are just barely tender, about 20 to 30 minutes, stirring gently occasionally (red lentils are very delicate). Stir in whatever meat or fowl is being used together with salt and pepper to taste. Cook only until soup is heated through, remembering the delicacy of the red lentils which will fall apart if overcooked.
Serve with a garnish of fresh chives, parsley or chopped fresh celery leaves on top.

Serves 6

TACO SOUP

Soooo easy! But so delicious! Try it!

1 lb. lean ground beef
1 medium onion, chopped
1 pkg. mild taco seasoning mix
1 can (14 oz.) pinto beans, rinsed and drained
3 cans (14 ozs.) stewed tomatoes
1 can (8 ozs.) tomato sauce
1 can (14 ozs.) whole kernel corn
1 cup grated cheddar or Monterey Jack cheese
1 pkg. (8 ozs.) corn chips, crushed slightly
1/2 cup sour cream

Saute' beef and onion in a deep fryer. Add the beans, tomatoes, corn, tomato sauce and taco seasoning mix and simmer for about 30 minutes.
Serve in bowls topped with grated cheese, corn chips and sour cream.

Serves 4 to 6

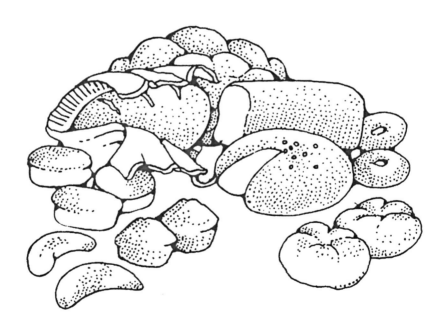

BREAD SUGGESTIONS

ALL PURPOSE CORN BREAD

1 1/2 cups unbleached all-purpose flour
1 cup yellow cornmeal
2 tsp. baking powder
1/4 tsp. baking soda
3/4 tsp. salt
1/4 cup packed light brown sugar
3/4 cup frozen corn kernels, thawed
1 cup buttermilk
2 large eggs
8 tbsp. (1 stick) unsalted butter, melted and cooled slightly

Adjust oven rack to middle position; heat oven to 400 degrees. Spray 8 inch square baking pan with cooking spray. Whisk flour, cornmeal, baking powder, baking soda, and salt in medium bowl until combined. Set aside.

In food processor or blender, process brown sugar, thawed corn kernels, and buttermilk until combined, about 5 seconds. Add eggs and process until well combined (corn lumps will remain,) about 5 seconds longer.

Using rubber spatula, make well in center of dry ingredients; pour wet ingredients into well. Begin folding dry ingredients into wet, giving mixture only a few turns to barely combine. Add melted butter and continue folding until dry ingredients are just moistened. Pour batter into prepared baking dish and smooth surface with spatula. Bake until deep golden brown and toothpick inserted in center comes out clean, 25 to 35 minutes.

Cool on wire rack 10 minutes; invert cornbread onto wire rack, then turn right side up and continue to cool until warm, about 10 minutes longer. Cut into pieces and serve.

Makes one 8-inch square.

SPICY JALAPEÑO-CHEDDAR CORNBREAD

Shred 4 ounces sharp cheddar cheese (about 1 1/3 cups.) Follow recipe above, reducing salt to 1/2 tsp. and add 3/8 teaspoon cayenne, 1 medium jalapeño chile, cored, seeded and chopped fine, and half of shredded cheddar to flour mixture in first step. Toss well to combine. Reduce sugar to 2 tbsp. and sprinkle remaining cheddar over batter in baking dish just before baking.

CROUTONS

The sourdough bread used in making these croutons makes all the difference in the final product.

2 cups small cubes of sourdough bread
3 tbsps. butter or more
2 tsps. sesame seeds
1/2 tsp. chili powder
salt to taste

In a heavy skillet on very low heat brown and stir all five ingredients until crisp. Be careful as the sesame seeds burn easily.

ITALIAN BREAD or PANE

This is the type of Italian bread used to make the now popular Panini, and you will find it easy to make, and adaptable to various other shapes than the one presented here.

2 envelopes dry yeast
about 3 cups lukewarm water
6 cups flour
1 tbsp. sugar
1 tbsp. salt
1/4 tsp. white pepper
1/4 cup olive oil
cornmeal
1 egg, beaten
sesame seeds (optional)

In a small bowl soften the yeast in 1/2 cup of the lukewarm water and combine it in a larger bowl with the dry ingredients and as much of the remaining warm water, or more, as may be needed to make a dough that is soft but not sticky. Work into it the olive oil and knead dough vigorously for 10 minutes or until it is quite elastic. Place dough in a slightly oiled bowl. Brush top of dough also with a little oil and cover it lightly with a cloth. Set bowl in a draft free place and allow it to rise until it has doubled in bulk (1 to 1 1/2 hours). When dough has risen as required, press it down and let it rise again until it has once more doubled in bulk. Press it down again and divide it into 3 equal parts. Shape each part into a round loaf about 7 inches in diameter. Lightly oil a baking sheet, sprinkle it with cornmeal, and arrange loaves on it. Set baking sheet in a warm place and let loaves rise for 30 minutes. Cut a cross about 1/4 inch deep into top of each loaf and let loaves rest 10 minutes longer. Preheat oven to 400 F. Brush loaves with the beaten egg and, if desired, sprinkle with sesame seeds. Bake loaves in preheated oven for 30 minutes or until golden brown and test done (tap loaves with fingers and if they sound hollow, they are baked). Place on wire rack to cool.

Makes 3 loaves

POTATOES-au-GRATIN BREAD

2 (1/4 oz.) pkgs. active dry yeast
   (2 tbsps.)
2 tbsps. sugar
1/2 cup warm water
1 cup half and half
3 tbsps. butter, melted

1 tbsp. salt
4 to 5 cups flour
2 cups shredded potatoes
1 cup shredded very sharp
   cheese (4 oz.)
2 tbsps. butter, melted

In large bowl of electric mixer, dissolve yeast and sugar in water. Let stand until foamy, (5 to 10 minutes). Add half and half, 3 tbsps. butter, salt, and 2 to 2 1/2 cups flour. Beat at medium speed with electric mixer 2 minutes (or 200 vigorous strokes by hand). Stir in potatoes and enough remaining flour to make a soft dough. Turn out dough onto a lightly floured surface. Clean and grease bowl. Knead dough 8 to 10 minutes or until smooth and elastic. If dough feels a little sticky, the starch in the potatoes is to blame. Do not worry. Place dough in greased bowl, turning to coat all sides. Cover with slightly damp towel and let rise in a warm place, free from drafts, until doubled in bulk, about 1 hour. Grease and flour 2 round 9 inch cake pans or 2 (1 1/2 quart) casserole bowls. Punch down dough. Pat into a rectangle, 1/2 inch thick. Sprinkle cheese over dough. Kneed cheese into dough until evenly distributed. Divide dough in half. Shape into 2 round loaves. Let rise until doubled in bulk, about 45 minutes. Preheat oven to 400 F. Slash tops of loaves to suit. Brush each loaf with 1 tbsp. melted butter. Bake 35 to 40 minutes, or until bread sounds hollow when tapped on the bottom. Remove from pans and cool on racks.

Makes 2 loaves.

This bread is even better the second day!

STOCKS

BEEF BROTH OR STOCK

4 lbs. beef soup bones (pieces)
2 1/2 qts. cold water
1 tsp. salt
1 bay leaf
2 sprigs parsley

1 medium onion, peeled
2 whole cloves
1 carrot, scraped
1 branch celery with leaves

Remove meat from bones and cut it in small pieces. Put meat, bones, water and remaining ingredients in a kettle (stick the cloves in the onion). Do not cover. Simmer for 3 hours. Strain. Reserve the meat for other recipes. Refrigerate overnight to remove fat from the broth, then skim off with knife and spoon.

To clarify broth, crush an egg shell and mix with 1 egg white and 1/4 cup cold water. Stir into lukewarm defatted broth. Heat to boiling, turn off heat and let stand about 5 minutes.
Strain through cheesecloth or fine sieve.

Makes 2 quarts

CHICKEN STOCK

10 lbs. chicken wings, backs and necks
2 whole cloves
2 large onions
4 carrots
2 leeks (white part and 1 inch of green only)
2 stalks or ribs of celery, with leaves
6 garlic cloves, unpeeled
1 cup fresh parsley sprigs (not cilantro)
1 tsp. dried rosemary, mashed with mortar and pestle
2 bay leaves
1/2 tsp. dried thyme
1/2 tsp. peppercorns

Cover chicken with water in stockpot. Bring to boil over medium heat, skimming surface as needed. Boil slowly for 2 hours, uncovered, skimming frequently. Stick cloves into 1 onion. Add to stockpot with all remaining ingredients, and simmer for 2 hours more, adding water as necessary to keep ingredients covered. Strain stock into heavy saucepan, and continue to simmer until reduced to 3 quarts. Cool and refrigerate, and discard fat from surface before using. This stock can be frozen for later use.

Makes about 3 quarts

FISH STOCK

If you can't find fish bones and heads, use an inexpensive, bony white fish such as whiting or catfish, but not an oily fish. And do not overdo the salt but, rather, add it to taste after the stock is made. Fish has considerable natural salt already.

2 lbs. fish bones and heads or
  2 lbs. bony fish
3 cups water
3 cups dry white wine
1 lemon slice
1 celery stalk or 3 tops
1 medium carrot, sliced

1 small onion stuck with 2
  cloves
1 tsp. fennel seeds
4 sprigs parsley
6 peppercorns, crushed
1 small bay leaf
1/2 tsp. thyme

Wash fish well and remove gills from heads. Combine in a pan with all other ingredients except salt. Bring to a boil. Reduce heat to simmer and cook 20 to 30 minutes. Taste and add salt to taste as needed.

Makes 6 cups

VEGETABLE BROTH OR STOCK

3 carrots, finely chopped
3 cups celery, finely chopped
3 onions, finely chopped
1/2 lb. mushrooms or mushroom
  stems sliced

3 leeks, sliced
3 qts. water
1 bay leaf
salt

Combine the carrots, celery, onions, mushrooms, leeks, water and a bay leaf in a pan. Bring to a boil, reduce heat and simmer, covered, for 2 1/2 hours. Strain the broth, discarding the vegetables, and season to taste with salt.

Makes 3 quarts

GLOSSARY

GLOSSARY

HERB BLENDS:

For soups in general: 2 parts each thyme or summer savory, parsley, chervil, basil, sweet marjoram, celery or lovage leaves

One part each sage, rosemary, dried ground lemon peel

Herb salt: 1 tsp. garlic salt, 2 tsps onion salt, 1 tsp. dry parsley. Possible additions — 1/2 tsp. basil, 1/2 tsp. marjoram

Fish Herbs blend: 1 part each tarragon, basil, marjoram, chervil and parsley

Note: To release flavors of the herbs, grind them in a mortar with salt or with herb salt if you are using it along with other herb groups

GENERAL MEASUREMENTS:

Beans: **1 cup dried = 3 cups cooked**
1 cup split peas = 2 1/4 cups cooked
1 cup lentils = 2 to 2/14 cups cooked (if using red lentils, remember to cook them for less time to avoid crumbling as reds are very delicate)

Beans included are black, black eyed peas, garbanzo, white, kidney, navy and lima.

Rice: 1 cup white = 3 cups cooked
Cheese: 4 ozs. = 1 cup shredded
1 cup brown = 3 to 4 cups cooked
1 cup converted = 4 cups cooked

Pasta: 1 cup macaroni = 1 1/3 to 2 1/4 cups cooked
1 cup egg noodles = 1 1/4 cups cooked

ABBREVIATIONS:

Tablespoon = tbsp.   Teaspoon = tsp.   Pound = lb. Ounce = oz.

GARAM MASALA:

3 tbsps. (about 20) black, or (75) green cardamom pods
3 cinnamon sticks, 3 inches long
1 tbsp. whole cloves
1/4 cup black peppercorns
1/2 cup cumin seeds
1/2 cup coriander seeds

Break open cardamom pods. Remove seeds and reserve. Discard the skin. Crush cinnamon with a kitchen mallet or rolling pin to break it into small pieces. Combine all the spices, and grind them. Then heat a heavy frying pan, preferably iron, for 2 minutes over medium heat. Add the spices and roast over medium heat, stirring and shaking the pan constantly in order to prevent burning. Do not allow the spices to burn, which they will do very quickly once the moisture has dried out. Roast them until they are dark brown. If necessary, turn down the heat a little. When brown, around 8 to 10 minutes usually, remove from pan at once and cool in a clean, dry bowl. The garam masala is now complete. This recipe may be made in a half batch.

CILANTRO CREME

Big handful of cilantro
2 tbsps. milk
1/2 cup sour cream
Pinch of salt or to taste

Blend the cilantro with the milk. When it is well blended add the sour cream and salt. Blend to mix, adding more sour cream if needed to thicken. Do not overblend or sour cream will break up.

INDEX

404177

Made in the USA